PRAISE FO

PRIESTS DE LA RÉSISTANCE

'A fascinating and entirely benign book, imbued with a surprisingly muscular Christianity and full of stories you may not know but which need to be heard.'

Spectator Books of the Year

'[T]his winter's best title is Fergus Butler-Gallie's work on wartime heroics by the clergy.'

Patrick Kidd, *The Times*

'This book is a gripping story of bravery, derring-do and cunning in the face of Fascism...vividly told tales of fifteen people who became caught up in the struggles against Fascism in Europe in the 1930s.'   *Tablet*

'Fifteen short, engaging essays... The reverend is a good writer with a light touch, and a natural storyteller.'

New Statesman

'It is refreshing to read an unashamedly admiring study of priests and ministers who have put their lives on the line... readable and moving.'   *BBC History Magazine*

'A timely and uplifting book... An hugely enjoyable if slightly eccentric account of clerical heroism in the face of evil... [Butler-Gallie] achieves an inspiring effect through the sheer cumulative impact of so many brave decisions.'

Julian Coman, *Observer*

'Here the Reverend Butler-Gallie wittily profiles fifteen "loose cannons" who stood up against fascism.' *Strong Words*

'Butler-Gallie serves them and their stories well with background information, a fluent narrative style, and a fine eye for the quirky and telling personal or historical detail.' *Church Times*

'A field guide to 20th-century priests, monks and nuns from all over the world who were prepared to die for their faith and to die saving others... He proves it true that comedy and tragedy run side by side, and that some of the most unlikely people turn out to be saints and martyrs... Bracing and lively.' *The Times*

'As entertaining as it is erudite, this enthralling anthology presents a cornucopia of quirky, courageous Fascist-fighting clerics.' LoveReading

PRIESTS
DE LA
RÉSISTANCE!

The Loose Canons Who Fought Fascism
in the Twentieth Century

THE REVD
FERGUS BUTLER-GALLIE

ONEWORLD

A Oneworld Book

First published by Oneworld Publications, 2019
This paperback edition published in 2021

ISBN 978-1-78607-830-8
eISBN 978-1-78607-673-1

Illustration credits: Dietrich Bonhoeffer © Chronicle/Alamy;
Churchill and Damaskinos © Dmitri Kessel/The LIFE Picture
Collection/Getty; Jane Haining © Historic Images/Alamy;
Pastor Fred Shuttlesworth and Dr King © Bettmann/Getty

Typeset by Fakenham Prepress Solutions, Fakenham, Norfolk NR21 8NL

Printed and bound in Great Britain by Clays Ltd, Elcograf S.p.A.

Oneworld Publications
10 Bloomsbury Street
London WC1B 3SR
England

Stay up to date with the latest books,
special offers, and exclusive content from
Oneworld with our newsletter

Sign up on our website
oneworld-publications.com

To my grandparents, who lived through the dark times herein described, and who helped foster in me two great loves – of history and of hope.

CONTENTS

INTRODUCTION

War, Witness & Where We Are Now

There is a story that echoes around the beer halls of Prague. It's as much part of the atmosphere as the folds of tobacco smoke and the groups of old men invariably huddled in the corner (who will, if the reader is prepared to pay for a round of drinks, relate the tale themselves – replete with a sworn affidavit that they knew people who saw it happen – despite the fact that it was almost certainly the invention of a Czech novelist). The story tells of an incident during the Nazi occupation of Prague, not long after the appointment of Reinhard Heydrich, the Director of the Gestapo, as 'Protector' of Bohemia and Moravia in 1941. Heydrich was perhaps the most zealous member of the whole Nazi leadership – even Hitler commented on his absolute lack of pity, referring to the tall Saxon as 'the man with the iron heart'. He was utterly committed to the ideology of Nazism and his rule in Prague was supposed to be a 'dry run' for how newly conquered territories would be administered when the inevitable total victory of Fascism was achieved. Heydrich set about his task with great enthusiasm, displaying a callous, urbane efficiency in consigning both places and people to oblivion.

A key part of Heydrich's programme was to demonstrate the superiority of the Reich's Teutonic culture over all
others – but especially over the 'degenerate' Slavic and Jewish
cultures, both of which were in abundant evidence in the city
of Prague. As befits the birthplace of *Don Giovanni*, Prague is
home to myriad opera houses, musical theatres and concert
halls. Perhaps the grandest of these is the Rudolfinum, a
barn of a building, its roof ringed by statues of the great
composers who have looked out sullenly on the River Vltava
since the late nineteenth century. Heydrich, so the story
goes, became aware that among these inanimate virtuosi
there was a stone Mendelssohn, a composer despised by the
Führer on account of his Jewish birth. Consequently, the
Reichsprotektor ordered the removal and destruction of the
offending sculpture. A group of soldiers were dispatched to
the concert hall accordingly, only to be met with tight-lipped
silence as to which of the statues was, in fact, Mendelssohn
from the building's Czech curators (who, incidentally, will
of course have been regulars in whichever pub the reader
chooses to have the tale related to them). Frustrated, the
soldiers used good Nazi logic and, after some searching,
sourced a tape measure with which they proceeded to
measure the noses of each of the statues. Having established
which symphonist had the most sizeable conk, they began
to have it removed, only for an onlooker to shout up that
the figure they were in fact removing was Richard Wagner,
Hitler's favourite composer.

The verisimilitude of the tale aside, it does highlight
certain aspects of Fascism that are undoubtedly true.
Foremost is its phenomenal pettiness. That one of the most
senior officials of what was supposed to be a Thousand-Year
Reich, destined to stretch across continents and radically
change human society forever, decided to take time out of

his day to fuss over the cosmetics of a music hall is astonishing. It is one of the reasons why Fascist figures, from Chaplin's *The Great Dictator* to *South Park*'s Eric Cartman, have consistently been considered so bathetic. It is hard not to laugh at the banality of it all. And yet that banality is, as Hannah Arendt so famously pointed out, one of the most chilling things about totalitarian ideology. To fuss over the identities of a set of sixty-year-old statues is ludicrous, but to do it and then calmly order the slaughter of thousands of human beings is deeply disturbing. It is a tendency that has outlasted the particular incarnation of totalitarianism described above – from the arcane and complex ranks of the Ku Klux Klan to the propensity of dictators to pursue personal vendettas against people of proportionately little importance. Given this focus on minutiae, by equal measures amusing and appalling, it is not surprising that much resistance to Fascism consists of small acts of defiance – the smuggled loaf of bread, the individual refusal to salute, the one life saved. One tiny act of resistance is enough to prove that the totalitarian's victory is not, in fact, total, that they will never conquer everything.

Secondly, and in seeming contrast, it shows us the enormous credence Fascism gives to its own historical and cultural narrative and the necessarily vast scope of said narrative. This is, of course, not something unique to Fascist movements – almost every ideological child of the French Revolution (whose adherents, lest we forget, tried to actually bring about Year Zero, creating a new calendar with days named after fruit baskets and crayfish) has sought to rewrite history as inexorably leading to the moment of glory. The slight problem with this historiographical exercise is that one comes up against things, ideas, people, etc. that do not necessarily match up to one's expectations. Such a scenario presents two options: either you bend said obstacles to fit the narrative or attempt to remove them altogether. Either choice would be a tall order for anyone, let alone neurotic, external-decor-obsessed Teutons or tubby, bedsheet-wrapped Midwesterners, yet, be it through the mediation of the *Kulturkammer* or the misinformation of Fake News, this rewriting and reshaping of narrative is invariably a key part of Fascist projects.

Fascism is, broadly speaking, a phenomenon of the West and, of the skeletons in the West's cultural cupboard, there can be little doubt that Christianity looms as one of the largest. The relationship between Christianity and Fascism is an inordinately complex one and the topic of many a weightier tome than this. Undeniably, Christians have been complicit in the projects of Fascism, in both its rewriting of the past and its horrific attempts to fashion a new future. Often, Christianity is seen as a pliant, client religion whose historic association with the cultures of the West makes it an easily co-opted ally. From the Ustaše of Croatia to the Reich Church in Germany, from activists of the past to apologists today, there are plenty of examples of Christians, lay and ordained, who have either convinced themselves that collaboration with and propagation of political systems that express themselves through radical, exclusivist authoritarianism serves the establishment of the Kingdom of God or that 'render unto Caesar that which is Caesar's' gives carte blanche for silence in the face of persecution of God's children. Crucially, this book does not seek to minimise these problematic figures but, by drawing attention to those who acted so differently, to show how wrong they were and continue to be.

There are those within Fascist movements (and, indeed, many other totalitarian ideologies) too who have made

4

considerable attempts to bend Christianity to be that pliant and easy ally. Nazism held Christianity to be fundamentally a distraction from its goals, but one that could at times be useful. The Nazis famously suggested that women focus on the three Ks – *Kinder, Küche, Kirche* (children, kitchen, church). It is testament to their views on Christianity that it didn't occur to them that it was precisely because of dedication to Church and children that a number of women made the decision to actively oppose the horrors of the regime. Nobody, to the author's knowledge, entered into resistance against Fascism for culinary reasons (although Canon Félix Kir, of Kir Royale fame, undoubtedly had strong opinions on the superiority of French cuisine). In private, Hitler expressed scorn for the 'meekness and flabbiness' of the Christian faith and vowed that one day he would 'have the Church on the ropes', a day that, in part due to people acting on the meek and flabby precepts of Christianity, never came.

Latter-day Fascism (be it in Hungary, France or the United States) has made more of a concerted effort to enlist Christianity in its appeals and statements. Yet invariably it is appealed to as an ethnographic identity rather than a religious one – with modern-day proponents of Fascism seeking to defend Western Christendom from its enemies. There are two particularly delicious ironies in this. Firstly, according to most estimates, between 60 and 70 per cent of all Christians now live outside the West: Nigeria has more than double the number of Protestants that Germany has and Brazil has well over double Italy's number of Roman Catholics. The West hasn't been as non-Christian as it is now since the Dark Ages – the Global South, by contrast, has never been more Christian than it is today. To identify Christianity as Western, therefore, is a bit like identifying football as English – yes, there are historic links, but its homeland is really nothing to shout about. Secondly, since the days of St Paul, Christianity has had a lack of internal ethnic distinction as a key tenet of its teaching (if not, regrettably, always of its practice). Paul wrote that 'there is neither Jew nor Greek, slave nor free, male nor female; all are one in Christ'. Indeed, a key part of Christianity's demographic success and a core explanation as to why it gave birth to the secular ideologies of the Enlightenment was its stated rejection of the idea that righteousness or truth belonged to any particular ethnographic grouping.

Inevitably, however, both the Fascists of the past and of today contrived and continue to contrive intellectual gymnastics to try and get past these tenets and, just as inevitably, they came up against and continue to come up against the figure of Jesus Christ. Firstly, they have to explain away his teachings: 'Love thy neighbour as thyself', 'Blessed are the peacemakers', the parables of the prodigal son, the unmerciful servant and of the Good Samaritan are all pretty considerable stumbling blocks to any political system based on the narrowing of neighbourliness, the refusal to forgive and forget and the propagation of arbitrary violence. But they also come up against him in thousands of ordinary Christians who did and still do take those teachings to heart. They came up against the figure of Christ in the bombastic priest who blew up Nazi fortifications in a Resistance jailbreak; in the imperious Archbishop who openly condemned their treatment of Jews and facilitated the escape and hiding of thousands; in the young seminarian who took a bullet intended for a young black girl whose only crime had been to try and go to school; as the hand of the Scots spinster-missionary calmly held that of a frightened Hungarian child as their train drew into

Auschwitz. This book is a collection of some of those stories and is written in hope that, should Fascism rear its head in the West once more, it might come up against the figure of Christ again.

RESISTANCE PAR EXCELLENCE

'I cannot turn my coat ...'

FRANCE

— CANON FÉLIX KIR —

White Wine & Espionage

It was a crisp September morning when the moment the people of Dijon had awaited for over four years finally came. The Second World War had not been easy for the Burgundian capital. It had seen more than its fair share of violence, sitting as it did near both the demarcation line of Vichy France and the border with the region of Alsace-Lorraine, which Hitler had symbolically reincorporated into the homeland of the German Reich. From German mass executions and Vichy-assisted deportations to acts of sabotage by the Resistance and aerial bombardment by the US Air Force – Dijon had seen it all and now, finally, at about a quarter past nine on 11th September 1944, the end of those horrors, the forthcoming moment of liberation was so close that her citizens could almost taste sweet freedom once more.

Tasting aside (and anyone who has sampled a spoonful of Dijon's eponymous mustard or been anywhere near the infamous regional specialty of an *andouillette* will know that the Burgundians are not ones for subtle flavours), they could certainly hear it. The city had been abandoned by the

German forces in order that they might concentrate their efforts on the defence of the Reich and on the forthcoming counter-attack in the Ardennes. They had also destroyed the town's railway lines four days earlier, meaning that the liberating forces approached the expectant denizens of Dijon by road and were able to drive a large squadron of tanks in open order towards the city, with engines roaring, crews happily chattering, and minimal resistance. In line with the policy insisted upon at the liberation of other major cities by the de facto French leader General de Gaulle, the first troops to set foot in the newly freed Dijon were to be French and the first flag to be hoisted was not to be the Union Flag or the Stars and Stripes but the Tricolore. Although Allied High Command agreed to the terms set out by de Gaulle, they did, perhaps tellingly, order an American armoured division to follow a few miles behind, in case anything got hairy. And so the stage had been set for a great propaganda moment as Free Frenchmen freed Frenchmen. However, de Gaulle and the French military were to have their limelight stolen, not by General Patton nor even by Hitler, but by an altogether more formidable, if somewhat unlikely, figure.

As the noise of the approaching tanks became louder, some of the good folk of Dijon could no longer contain themselves and, rushing past ruined shops and bombed-out homes, made their way to meet the liberation column. The sight that met them was nothing short of extraordinary. For a start, many of the troops were soldiers from France's African colonies, their distinctive red fezzes and elaborately faced overcoats as unfamiliar to the denizens of landlocked, provincial Dijon as their black skin. However, their appearance was positively unremarkable compared to the figure who sat atop one of the tanks as it trundled into the city. The role of Caesar in this mechanised triumph was played by Canon Félix Kir – priest, politician, Resistance hero, and world-famous consumer of alcohol. Wearing his priest's cassock, his cloak billowing around him and his beret wedged firmly on his podgy, balding head (for, if there was one identity that mattered more to Kir than his priesthood, it was, as we shall see, the fact that he had been born a Frenchman), Canon Kir made his return to the city from which, a matter of months before, he had only just escaped with his life.

While the sight was undoubtedly an unusual one, the vision of the doughy, dimpled clergyman trying to maintain his balance on the bonnet of the clunking, camouflaged vehicle was as clear a sign that the horrors of Fascism had finally been defeated as any hoisting of a flag or singing of the 'Marseillaise'. Kir had been the embodiment of resistance in Dijon for the previous four and a half years. From daily acts of disobedience and subterfuge in his (self-appointed) role as a leader of the municipal community to his active role in Resistance sabotage of German military operations, Kir had stared death in the face for the cause of freedom in this corner of Burgundy a number of times. Now he was greeted as a hero.

In fact, Kir had spent the days since he had heard the news of the impending German abandonment of Dijon scurrying on foot over the sixty miles from his hiding place in a small town north-west of the city. When he heard that the French troops were due to roll into Dijon the following morning, Kir, who was, as we shall see, the master of the symbolic act, quickly arranged to secure a place atop a tank, allowing the photographers, journalists, and whoever it is that formulates the annals of local myth and legend, to capture him as the liberator of Dijon for posterity.

And thus was Dijon liberated – in scenes less like *Band of Brothers* and more like *'Allo 'Allo*. Ridiculous though he might appear from such a vignette, Kir was neither a clown nor a charlatan. While stealing the limelight at the liberation of his adopted home town shows his undoubted capacity for sly mischief, it also gives an indication of his sheer ballsiness. It was a character trait he held in spades and, whether it was his refusal to salute German officers or his participation in a jailbreak, his tricking Nazi officials into preserving Jewish property or his taking several bullets from a would-be Fascist assassin, it was one that he would demonstrate again and again during the hellish period of German occupation.

There can be little doubt about what imbued Kir with both such cunning and courage: he had an unwavering faith in himself, no doubt, but, much more than that, he had a staunch faith in Christ. Inevitably, the French Resistance was a somewhat ragtag collection of individuals united by their commitment to fighting Fascism. Through it, Kir found himself routinely having to make common cause with ardent Marxists who decried all forms of religious belief. Kir became used to fielding questions about how it was he could possibly believe in a God that he couldn't see, honing an answer that he deployed in response to many an atheist during his later political career: 'Well, you can't see my arse and yet we know it exists!'

In the Gospel according to St Matthew, Christ sends out his disciples with the instruction to be 'wise as serpents and innocent as doves'. There was undoubtedly an innocence, a childlike quality almost, to Kir's dogmatic faith and yet, as many a German officer or Fascist collaborator found to their detriment, there was also the cunning wisdom of a serpent and the bravery of a lion in the old canon as well.

Félix Kir was born in January 1876, in the little town of Alise-Sainte-Reine, a commune of a few hundred souls halfway between the gold-green vine-covered slopes of Chablis and the sprawling bricks and mortar of Dijon. Kir's father was one Jules Kir, the small town's flamboyant jack of all trades – fulfilling the roles of hairdresser, apothecary, doctor and nurse for its citizens. Young Félix learned from him two things: firstly, that the ability to walk into a situation with a supreme self-confidence qualified one to perform any job, regardless of such petty considerations as formal or legal qualifications; secondly, a deep, abiding love for France. The elder Kir's family had come to Alise a little earlier in the nineteenth century from the province of Alsace-Lorraine, the borderlands which had, just five years earlier, been ceded to the emergent German Empire in the Franco-Prussian War. As a child, the maps in young Félix's school were depicted with 'the black stain', where the 'stolen' territories were painted over with a thick black paint. French children of his generation were taught not to forgive and not to forget.

Along with his charismatic father, another figure who shaped the consciousness of the young Félix was the Gaulish chieftain Vercingetorix, who had been executed by Julius Caesar more than one thousand nine hundred years earlier. Vercingetorix quite literally loomed large in young Félix's life. Eleven years before he had been born, the then French Emperor Napoleon III had ordered the erection of an enormous statue of the semi-naked Gaulish warrior (with a face modelled on his own) on the hillside above Alise-Sainte-Reine which had, as Aleisa, been the site of the Gauls' final defeat by Caesar in 52 BC. As he and his friends would re-enact the great clash of civilisations, the words from Caesar's own account of the battle that were inscribed at the base of the statue must have settled in Félix's febrile young mind: 'A united Gaul, forming a single nation, animated by a common spirit, can defy the Universe.' Love of his country, combined with a frankly pig-headed refusal to give in to any threat, was to become Félix Kir's signature character trait.

Félix was a bright, mischievous child and, in common with many of the more intelligent children of the lower middle classes, his route to an education that reflected his natural ability was through the schools run by the Church. His innate theatricality and sharp intellect meant that he was soon selected for ministry and, after a period of study at seminary in Dijon, was ordained a priest in 1901. The following twenty-seven years of his ministry consisted of the increasingly portly cleric pottering around the Burgundian countryside as parish priest in a succession of villages and small towns. Kir was well liked, and had his pastoral side, but he seemingly spent most of this time enjoying the region's distinctive cuisine and excellent wines (he was a stone's throw from Chablis, Beaune and Beaujolais), as well as disappearing with his bathing costume and dedicating entire summer days to floating lazily down the Ouche, a tributary of the Rhône that flows through the region. Although his bishop complained that he ought to move to Dijon itself and do some more quantifiable work (namely editing the diocesan newspaper), which somewhat shattered his rural idyll, Félix Kir's pre-war existence was hardly a taxing one. He became well known in Dijon itself, developing his distinctive beret-cassock dress combo and maintaining his thick, rural Burgundian accent, with its distinct, rolled 'r's lending a particular richness to his catchphrase as it echoed around Dijon's cafés and churches: 'Je vous offrrre un blanc de cassis.'

His work for the bishop paid off and he was given the honorary title of canon and became active as a representative of the national Catholic political movement in the region. His role took him across the regions of eastern France. When he travelled to give his speeches or celebrate Mass, he would sometimes take with him, among his other pieces of priestly paraphernalia, a case containing a bottle of the Burgundian Aligoté wine and a bottle of the blackcurrant liqueur cassis. His evangelistic task was twofold: to sell the cause of political Catholicism to the masses and to introduce their palates to his region's favourite tipple. Kir, proud of his nation, proud of his faith and proud of his region (and her alcoholic charms), was the picture of contentment in the years between the First and Second World Wars. But behind the easy charm and laid-back attitude was an increasingly calculating political brain. It would take a combination of both these aspects of his character to navigate the whirlwind that was about to be unleashed on Félix Kir's idyllic little corner of France.

Canon Kir was sixty-three when British Prime Minister Neville Chamberlain announced that both his nation and their French allies were at war with Nazi Germany in the early autumn of 1939. Many would be thinking about retirement at such an age, but Kir had been living the easy life since at least the turn of the last century, and his career as a Resistance fighter, politician, swindler and saboteur was only just about to begin. On Monday 17th June 1940, Marshal Pétain, newly appointed Premier of France, announced that fighting against the forces of Nazi Germany would have to cease, having contacted Adolf Hitler some hours previously to offer France's surrender. Not long before Pétain's announcement, Robert Jardillier, the Mayor of Dijon, hurriedly stuffed a few belongings into a suitcase, bundled them into a waiting car and, leaving some scribbled orders for his citizens to either evacuate or surrender, left for the town of Autun, where he stopped briefly before continuing south. Once safely within the *zone libre,* he became, despite the fact that he was ostensibly part of the left-wing Socialist party, a stalwart supporter of Pétain's collaborationist Vichy regime.

Abandoned by their supposed political leaders both nationally and locally, the people of Dijon now faced the prospect of being overrun by the oncoming German forces. A small group gathered to act as municipal representatives, namely an elderly army colonel, a professor of English literature, a retired merchant navy commander, the Head of Dijon's Chamber of Commerce – and Canon Kir. This motley collection of civic sort of dignitaries was hardly the Justice League. Yet it was to them that the administration of Dijon fell. Technically, the group had nominated Paul Bur, the bearded President of the Chamber of Commerce, as the mayor. However, it was not in the nature of Canon Kir to play second fiddle. Consequently, when the colonel commanding the first German regiment to arrive in the city made his way up to the mayor's office, he found, sitting amid the chaos of papers and other debris that the flight of Jardillier had left behind and, as ever, resplendent in his flowing clerical cassock, none other than Canon Félix Kir.

The jackbooted colonel marched down the room towards the ornate desk behind which the clergyman sat, his stare fixed ahead, like a bullfrog in black silk. Perhaps it was the shock of the invasion, the colonel doubtless thought, but, in fact, Kir was just getting ready to catch his fly. 'Heil Hitler!' shouted the colonel, expecting a formal surrender or similar. Instead, the priest behind the desk just kept on staring. 'Heil

Hitler,' the German repeated. Still nothing. Slightly bemused, the colonel decided to try a more human response – after all, Pétain's instructions had been for the French authorities to cooperate as peacefully as possible with the occupiers. Perhaps a little of the old Teutonic charm would ease the old cleric from his seat? He stuck out his hand. Kir looked dismissively at it and said nothing. By now even the disciplined exterior of the Wehrmacht's finest was beginning to crack in the face of this Gallic hauteur. In broken French, the colonel demanded an explanation for this manifestly rude behaviour, given that the city's authorities were hardly in a position to offer any form of resistance. Kir, steadily maintaining his steely stare, reprimanded the officer for his failure to knock on the mayoral door and proceeded to explain that Dijon was a city of the first rank and, as such, he would not shake hands with any officer 'below the rank of a general'. Whether a general was eventually found, or whether Kir made a rare climbdown to engage with the colonel, history does not record, but the incident set the tone for what was to be a tempestuous four years, pitching the fat, bibulous priest against the full might of the occupying forces.

Kir set about making life as difficult as possible for the Nazis. He made early contact with the Resistance, forging unlikely working relationships with all sorts of individuals – including a number of Communists to whom he had been famously rude during his career as a Catholic political figure. He even managed to persuade the other members of the ragtag municipal authority to follow his lead, with Paul Bur eventually resigning his role of mayor in 1942, protesting that he could not help in the running of a city 'where the French are shot every morning'. Kir and his colleagues ensured that Resistance fighters had places to hide, that shipments designated for the German troops stationed in the city mysteriously 'went missing' and that the citizens of Dijon could continue their love of rich cuisine through a thoroughly organised mass circumnavigation of German-imposed rationing. Although obfuscation was his preferred modus operandi, Kir was not beyond using his natural earthy charm to achieve his aims as well. The German officer in command of Dijon was shocked when one day he received a note from the normally irascible canon, politely suggesting a particular building for use as a space for storing military supplies. Pleased that it would save him the difficult and unpopular task of requisitioning space, and sensing a mellowing in the little black bullfrog's attitude to the occupiers, the German willingly consented to Kir's suggestion. The canon had, in fact, hoodwinked him again, persuading him to keep his stores in the city's synagogue, ensuring that it would not be demolished as per the orders of the Nazi high command. Kir arranged for the Torah and other artefacts to be hidden before making his suggestion and turning the building over to the German forces, making the Nazi commandant the unlikely saviour of Dijon's Jewish community's house of prayer. When, in 1945, survivors of the Holocaust returned to Dijon, they were able to call on Canon Kir, reclaim their holy books and return to the space in which they had worshipped prior to the hell that had been unleashed on them by Nazism. Almost no other community from the shattered remnants of European Jewry was able to do the same.

Kir eventually found himself involved more and more in the operations of the Resistance. In particular, he relished his role in an audacious scheme to liberate prisoners from the Longvic internment camp just down the road from Dijon. Slave labour was a key part of Nazi infrastructure from Calais to the edge of the Caucasus. Not only were political prisoners and captured Allied troops used in the construction of the Nazi death machine, they were also available to pliant local authorities for more menial tasks. The self-appointed clerical factotum of Dijon was not, as we know, renowned for his constructive 'live and let live' attitudes. However, as a result of his near-constant badgering, the Nazis eventually gave him access to the pool of labour available at Longvic, which predominately housed French prisoners of war.

Over the course of the summer of 1940, the sight of the frog-like cleric striding purposefully towards the great barbed-wire fences of the camp became a familiar one. He would arrive, be monumentally rude to the guards on duty and then present a series of requests printed on official mayoral headed notepaper (which, of course, he had no actual right to use) for men to be released for prolonged periods of work on increasingly extravagant infrastructure projects. The prison guards, assuming such audacity had been sanctioned by someone higher up the command chain, would consent, leaving the canon to turn on his heel and stride back towards Dijon, Pied Piper-like, with a train of confused prisoners behind him. Once they were safely 'at work' on projects (the end dates of which invariably never made their way to the camp commandant), Kir would arrange for some of the men to disappear, either reuniting them with their former comrades in arms in the Resistance or arranging for escape routes into the neutral nations of Spain or Switzerland.

It is thought that Kir's bold ploy helped to break out nearly five thousand prisoners over the course of the war. Given the sheer volume of men that Kir was requesting for his mysterious municipal projects, it was hardly a surprise that the Germans soon twigged that something was amiss.

With a number of Kir's Resistance escapees now being recaptured, the canon's complicity was discovered and, in a fit of rage, the German commander sentenced him to death. However, with an increasingly volatile French population in the region and a sense of the regard in which the doughty Kir was now held, the Nazi high command for the region decided, in the cold light of day, to imprison him instead. In the end, even this was transmuted to house arrest after barely three months, such was the influence and support that Kir had acquired during his period of unlikely prominence.

Félix Kir had not sipped his last blanc de cassis just yet.

†

When, after the war, it was suggested by an individual of a more placatory disposition that Canon Kir might take a more conciliatory approach to his politics, he pointed to his cassock and shot back, 'I cannot turn my coat – it's black on both sides.' By that time, he had learned the hard way that stubbornness gets you everywhere.

In 1943, he was briefly imprisoned a second time on the (well-founded and accurate) suspicion that he was still closely involved in operations, from gun-running to propaganda manufacture, for the Resistance. His second imprisonment gave him the perfect vantage point to watch with glee as British planes executed a bombing raid on the Longvic airfield, allowing another batch of prisoners to escape. Unable to remove the obstacle of Kir by legal prosecution, flattery or persuasion, the Gestapo turned to more violent methods. Wary of making a martyr and, no doubt, giving the consummate showman yet another public platform, they decided against a trial and execution. Instead, they recruited a number of young French Fascists, eager to please their German ideological allies, to do the dirty work and assassinate Kir, thus removing the troublesome priest once and for all. But wherever would they find him?

Kir was in the kitchen, fixing himself a snack, perhaps with a blanc de cassis on the side, at 9 p.m. on 26th January 1944, when the doorbell to his modest apartment rang. Unwilling to be separated from his evening collation, Kir allowed his housekeeper, Alice Cordier, to open the door. Raised voices could be heard, there was a scuffle and through the door of the kitchen burst a masked youth who, with a cry of 'Retribution!', fired five shots at the canon. Lying on the floor, Kir made a calculation; he knew that he had been hit at least twice and was aware that the magazine would contain a sixth bullet which, if administered at close range, would undoubtedly kill him. Whether it was a stroke of quasi-theological genius, fight or flight kicking in, or just the effect of an evening on the cassis, Kir summoned all his strength and, with a great noise, hauled himself up so that he was facing his attackers head-on. Convinced that they had just witnessed a miraculous resurrection, the collabo-rators made like the Roman soldiers in the Garden and fled. In fact, Kir was badly wounded and bleeding heavily. Mme Cordier managed to contact some of the clergyman's fellow Resistance members and have him spirited away to the Sainte-Marthe hospital, where it was discovered that only the presence of his wallet, filled with papers to help him circumnavigate the authorities, had prevented a bullet from hitting his heart. The wallet was not the only thing that had stopped the bullets meant for Kir – the stove on which the canon was cooking up his late-night snack subsumed the other shots. Kir kept the piece of ragged kitchen equipment as a memento, often showing it to official visitors when he later became mayor.

Wartime Dijon was a hub of spies and double agents and it didn't take long for the news of the failed assassination and the truculent canon's presence in the hospital to come to the attention of the Gestapo, who sent a group of henchmen to finish the job. By the time they arrived, however, Kir was gone, spirited away in the dead of night and taken on a gruelling journey across the Burgundian countryside to a Resistance safe house (itself an impressive achievement for an overweight man in his late sixties who had just been shot). There he spent the following months recuperating until his re-enactment of another biblical incident – namely the Triumphal Entry – in September that year.

The people of Dijon did not forget Kir's leadership in their most trying hour. In 1945, he was elected both Mayor of Dijon (officially this time) and as an MP for the wider region and awarded the *Légion d'honneur*, France's highest decoration, begrudgingly bestowed by General de Gaulle, who would never forgive the canon for his scene-stealing cameo during Dijon's liberation. The authorities also pursued, arrested and eventually executed the men (whom Kir always referred to in later years as 'those Fascist fuckers') responsible for the shooting of the cleric (and his stove) back in 1944.

The memory of his singular bravery never faded, ensuring him re-election without any challenge by Gaullists or Socialists until his death in 1968. He relished the limelight and ruled over Dijon as his personal fiefdom, routinely making use of his mayoral privilege to force traffic policemen to hand over their distinctive white batons and hats, evicting them from their podiums, in order to play havoc with the city's traffic by way of amusement. He even found time to actually complete some of the extravagant infrastructure projects for which he'd requisitioned all that manpower during the war. One such was the construction of a large lake at his favourite bathing spot along the Ouche, which was, of course, christened 'Lake Kir'.

Kir's wartime experiences made him a great advocate for peace between nations. He was one of the first mayors in Europe to champion the twinning of towns, in particular reaching out to cities on the other side of the Iron Curtain. Given his own stoutly clericalist conservative views, he found an unlikely friend in the form of Nikita Khrushchev, who had helped keep up the spirits of another city that suffered the assaults of Nazism – Stalingrad. Khrushchev was intrigued by the tales of the gutsy cleric (and, as a Russian, was impressed by tales of his voluminous capacity for alcohol). The two exchanged letters and the Soviet leader even went so far as to visit Dijon during his trip to France in 1960. De Gaulle was apoplectic that the canon was about to steal his limelight again and so, when the car arrived to pick up the cleric turned mayor for Khrushchev's visit, the orders from the Élysée Palace were to instead drive an increasingly irate Kir in circles round the Burgundian countryside. In the end, the canon did get to meet his unlikely pen pal in Paris and, again, in 1964, when he was treated to the full force of Soviet hospitality on a trip to Moscow. Indeed, such was the strength of the link that the local Communist Party refused to field any candidate against Kir from then on.

Alongside his political commitments, Kir also maintained a vociferous interest in local Burgundian food and, more especially, drink. Well into his late eighties, Kir would take several hours over his lunch, almost always washed down by a blanc de cassis, a whole bottle of red and a slurp of sparkling white to finish, before – astonishingly – returning to his desk for an afternoon's work. He was notoriously fussy about the exact measures for an authentic blanc de cassis, even going so far as to pour every single drink out himself when a twinning delegation visited from Skopje in Macedonia and he discovered that the mayoral staff had prepared the town's speciality incorrectly. Indeed, such was his reputation for serving and consuming the drink that in 1951 a producer wrote to the canon to ask if they could market their version of the blanc de cassis as a 'Kir'. Unable to resist the offer of both self-publicity and ready access to complimentary alcohol, Kir happily consented and so a new phrase began to echo through the grand chambers of the Mayor's palace, still in that lilting Burgundian accent, of course: 'Je vous offrrre un Kirrrrrr?'

By the time he died, aged ninety-two and still Mayor of Dijon, he was a household name, not just in France but all over the world. To say that Canon Félix Kir was a man of many faces would be an understatement – he was a priest and a politician, a speechwriter and a spy, a wine-guzzler and a would-be martyr. He upstaged presidents and generals, hoodwinked commandants and put the fear of God into collaborators. He gave the Church over sixty-five years of ministry, he gave his nation decades of political service and he gave the world over half a century of blackcurrant and white wine hangovers. But far more impressive was his ministry to the people of Dijon in those troubled years of the Second World War. He gave them leadership, he gave them courage and, perhaps most importantly, he gave them hope. From saving synagogues to jailbreak coordination, all while slightly pissed, Kir was more than just a light in the darkness. He was a veritable firework bursting forth in the dark night-time of twentieth-century Europe.

In the Gospel according to St Matthew, Christ sends out his disciples with the instruction to be 'wise as serpents and innocent as doves'. Very few of those disciples can claim to have lived up to this instruction with quite the same bombastic *joie de vivre* as Canon Félix Kir.

— ABBÉ PIERRE —

The Miraculous Mountaineering Monk

It is one of the marks of the lingering presence of paganism that Christianity has never quite managed to divorce the idea of being 'blessed' with being 'lucky' even among its own followers. There is still a dynamic in the popular imagination that links blessing with good fortune, despite the fact that Jesus himself went around saying that those who were 'blessed' were people like the poor in spirit, the meek and those who mourn. Not exactly the types of people who get photographed holding an enormous novelty cheque. Indeed, if it were to be suggested that a naïve, socially unaware man plagued by ill health, who had barely survived persecution, shipwreck and plane crash was 'blessed', one might expect a deal of incredulity from even the most devout Christian. But Henri Marie Joseph Grouès, also known as Abbé Pierre (and, for a brief period, as 'Meditative Beaver'), had an undeniable aura that people routinely described as 'blessed'. And, to numerous people, from the terrified Jews trying to flee across the Alps to the thousands of homeless people eventually helped by his 'Emmaus' programme, he was also a source of blessing.

Having started as an awkward and gangly young would-be monk who only really found solace when he was climbing things, he ended his career the most respected and popular man in France. His journey saw him chased across deserts, seas and mountain ranges; it made of him a soldier, a forger and a political titan.

He was born in August 1912 into a colourful family in Lyon. An aunt was the infamous Héra Mirtel, a novelist, feminist and occultist who, when young Henri was eight years old, murdered her husband and then proceeded to send his body round the French rail network in a large trunk. Only when it began to leak blood onto other bags in the left luggage room at Nancy railway station was her crime found out. Henri's immediate family was only marginally less strange. His father was a wealthy silk merchant whose hobby was giving impromptu haircuts and shaves to members of Lyon's poorest neighbourhoods. Henri would routinely accompany his father on these bizarre trips, leading to a lifelong affection for the plight of the poor, as well as a lifelong aversion to shaving his beard, resulting in a somewhat bedraggled appearance in later years.

Overzealous paternal grooming aside, the teenage Henri grew up to be a remarkably handsome young man. With his chiselled jaw, athletic physique and piercing blue-grey eyes, he caught the attention of a number of women. Despite his shyness, and the fact that he wanted to become a monk, Henri was receptive to such attentions, a trope that continued well after his priestly ordination and his supposed vow of chastity. When, in later life, he inadvisably published a warts-and-all autobiography, he revealed that he hadn't exactly been assiduous in keeping to the celibate lifestyle either before or after he was ordained. Such an admission didn't, of course, make him popular with the Roman Catholic hierarchy (despite the fact that he was in good company – Saint Augustine's *Confessions* doesn't exactly stint on the details of his sex life), but it did further entrench him in the hearts of the French people, being, as they are, not a nation renowned for their suppression of sexual appetites.

Henri was most happy in his own company – a trait that found expression in two ways. One was in a love for the great outdoors; he would make regular trips to the nearby Alps and became an accomplished mountaineer, a skill that was to stand him in good stead later on. He was also an avid scout, leading a troop and, by the odd rules of nomenclature that govern the world of such uniformed organisations, was given the title 'Meditative Beaver', a reference to his quiet and contemplative persona. The second way in which his introverted nature found an expression was in his religious devotion, specifically in his vocation to become a monk. Unlike his cabbalist aunt, both Henri's parents were devout Catholics and had made sure he was educated by the Jesuits in Church schools. Despite his active lifestyle, Henri's health was never especially good. As a sixteen-year-old he was sent, at some considerable expense to his parents, to the seaside resort of Cannes, to recuperate from a lung infection (a condition that would affect him for the rest of his life). There, he was free from the ministrations of the Jesuits and able to spend the long hours of convalescence browsing the bookshelves of a different religious order – namely the Franciscans – where he found a life of St Francis himself. The tale of the son of a wealthy merchant for whom the appeal of the natural world helped him discern a call to the monastic life had obvious resonances. His parents were overjoyed, but, at sixteen, he was considered too young for the rigours of the monastery. A year and a half later, the monks of the Capuchin order (an offshoot of the Franciscans after whose distinctive habits both the capuchin monkey and cappuccino coffee are named) accepted him into their community in the town of Saint-Étienne. Henri renounced his worldly goods, his eccentric family and his name, becoming 'Brother Philippe'. And so, in the end, the vocation to the monastic life won out over the charms of the mademoiselles of Lyon or the challenging majesty of the mountains.

The rigours of monastic life, however, did not suit the newly minted Brother Philippe; dank stone, hard beds and early mornings didn't do his long-running health problems any favours and so he soon made preparations to leave the monastery and become an ordinary parish priest, despite his comparative lack of a formal theological education. Except 'ordinary', like 'lucky', is not an epithet that one would readily award to the life of Henri Grothis. Having been ordained priest in August 1938, not long after his twenty-sixth birthday, he took up the role as an assistant cleric at St Joseph's Church in the city of Grenoble, nestled at the foot of the Alps, in early 1939. His time there was short. Only a matter of months later, war was declared and the tall, contemplative cleric joined thousands of other men of his generation and was mobilised by the French army in preparation for war with Nazi Germany. Groise' clerical status was irrelevant to the avowedly secular French state and so he was called up like anyone else; what was more pertinent to his ability to fight for the country was his health. Ironically, the man who would become one of the most famed heroes of the French Resistance actually spent the duration of the official war between France and Germany laid up in a military hospital with a debilitating bout of pleurisy.

It was at a military hospital in Alsace that Brother Philippe heard of the surrender of French forces in May 1940. Not long after the announcement, he was discharged and made his way back through a quiet and conquered country to take up a role as chaplain to a hospital and orphanage in Grenoble. In October 1940, as he looked out of the train window towards the snow beginning to reclaim the slopes of his beloved Alps, Brother Philippe probably imagined that, for him, the war was over. How wrong he was.

†

On 18th July 1942, Brother Philippe made contact with a Free French operative working in Grenoble and announced that he wished to join the Resistance. In the time since his return to Grenoble, he had noticed growing persecution of Jewish people as well as political or social opponents of the Vichy regime, as the collaborators sought to demonstrate their commitment to working with the Nazis. The final straw for the young priest was the news from Paris of the Vel' d'Hiv Roundup – one of the most infamous events in France during the Second World War. Over the course of 16th and 17th July 1942, more than thirteen thousand Jews whose French citizenship was in doubt were rounded up by French police acting under Nazi orders. They were crammed into a series of confined spaces across Paris, with the majority herded into the Vélodrome d'Hiver, or Vel' d'Hiv, a winter cycling track not far from the Eiffel Tower. The space that had been the playground for the city's bright young things in the heady interwar years now became a scene of horror as vast numbers of terrified people were confined there without food, drink or basic sanitation. In the end, the French handed their Jewish internees over to the Nazis, who stated that they would be shipped east for 'resettlement'. The complicity of his countrymen in this act enraged Brother Philippe, by now an assistant priest at the cathedral in the centre of Grenoble. The very next day, he presented himself to the Resistance, determined that he at least would put up a fight against the horrors that were unfolding across Europe. The services he offered were his prominent public position, his mountaineering skills honed in his childhood and a quite astonishing reserve of courage.

Brother Philippe's work with the Resistance began almost immediately. He had long been involved in schemes to take care of the poor and destitute in Grenoble; now he turned his attention to those facing persecution as the raids on Jews extended south. He sourced access to a printing press and aided in the distribution of false documents to enable Jews, in particular Jewish children, to escape to Switzerland. The press came in useful for propaganda too as he turned his hand to editing and writing, setting up a newspaper (using yet another pseudonym, Monsieur Georges) to be distributed clandestinely to areas where there was hope that resistance could be fomented. Sometimes the figures he was helping were too well known to the Nazi or Vichy authorities for documents, forged or otherwise, to be much use and so other measures had to be considered. The former scout turned cleric, his health concerns taking a back seat to his iron determination, would help guide Resistance fighters and refugees through the passages and valleys that he had come to know so well through the Alps to eventual safety in neutral Switzerland. All the while, he maintained his parish responsibilities in Grenoble – mountaineering one minute and saying Mass the next. Indeed, such was the extent of his Resistance activity that, within the first year of joining, it became clear that he needed a code name to conceal his identity from German counter-agents, and so, the man who had been born Henri Grouès changed his name again and took on the appellation that would make him famous: Abbé Pierre.

In November 1942, the final illusion of French independence was shattered as the Germans took over military control of the southern part of the country – partly in response to the scale of Resistance efforts that were based there, including those of Abbé Pierre. Conscious that Fascism would not be defeated by philanthropy and kindness alone, Abbé Pierre joined in the formation of one of the hundreds of guerrilla groups (known as Maquis after the scrubland in which they often operated) that had sprung up across France in order to take the fight to the Nazis. The Abbé's first Maquis cell was based in the Chartreuse Mountains north of Grenoble, home to the order of Carthusian monks whose primary activities are silence and the production of the lurid, herbal hangover inducer of the same name. Abbé Pierre was not, however, interested in the Chartreuse for spiritual reasons of either kind – rather, he recognised that the isolated mountainous region would make the perfect training ground for the ragtag group of nationalists, Communists, anarchists and prisoners of war who were to make up his secret army. From November 1942, he began coordinating large-scale robberies of military stores from Nazi warehouses, always ensuring that any food or clothing taken was split between his own Resistance forces and the ordinary people of the surrounding area, by now feeling the full force of wartime privation.

By early 1943, Abbé Pierre was de facto coordinator for much of the Resistance against the Nazis and their Italian Fascist allies in the south-eastern corner of France. His role meant that he was constantly on the move to avoid detection by the Gestapo, who had not taken long to work out that Abbé Pierre and Brother Philippe were the same man. He routinely found himself camping out in the wilderness with fellow Maquis members as he trained them or billeted with the quietly brave French men and women who made up the majority of the Resistance.

One such woman was Lucie Coutaz, a secretary and committed churchgoer who sheltered Pierre during the early months of 1943. Theirs was to become a dynamic relationship, leading to the founding of the Emmaus charity, and undoubtedly they loved each other. Whether that was platonic or whether Lucie was whom the Abbé was referring to when he confessed to finding celibacy impossible, we shall never know, but we do know that they became an inseparable and formidable team as the Abbé darted across the south of France, training guerrillas, publishing propaganda, smuggling people to safety and, from time to time, saying Mass.

†

A figure in black scuttled across the empty square in Lyon. It was a scalding-hot day in the late summer of 1943 and, as any cleric knows, the black woollen cassock is not the most forgiving of outfits when temperatures rise. Sweat poured from the seminarian's brow as he entered the shade afforded by the stone vaults near one of the city's ancient Gothic churches, but this perspiration had almost nothing to do with the heat; the clergyman was carrying on his person pictures that would have resulted in his immediate execution. He was a young German trainee cleric, recently arrived in France via the Swiss border, and he was in Lyon to see Father Henri Grouès, alias Abbé Pierre. The French priest had already acquired a reputation for daring acts of bravado against the Nazis that had spread throughout clerical resistance groups and he was now prominent enough for his nervous German colleague to seek his advice.

In the cool backroom of a café, the German finally showed Pierre the contents of the package. It was a series of photographs, smuggled out using the Church's network, of the death camps operating in Poland. At first, the Frenchman refused to believe his eyes. He would later say, in shame at his own disbelief, that murder on such a scale seemed 'unthinkable' even for the Nazis. In the end, he was persuaded; the pictures confirmed the rumours that had circulated in Resistance groups since the opening of Treblinka, a year prior to the Abbé's meeting in Lyon. The Jews whose arrests had so angered the young priest a year previously had not been sent for resettlement at all but to be murdered on a mass and mechanised scale.

Pierre was supposed to be in Lyon keeping a low profile after Gestapo agents in Grenoble had sussed out his illicit activity in the areas around the Alps. However, he had kept up contact with another Maquis cell in the wild Pilat region just south of Lyon and, spurred on by the horror of the images he had been shown by the German, doubled down to begin waging nothing short of open war on the Nazis – a mission that would take him across two continents, earn him several new nicknames and see him stare death in the face more than once.

Abbé Pierre did not have to wait long for the opportunity to pull off an iconic set piece. The autumn of 1943 saw a concerted German crackdown on the Free French resistance, as Hitler became increasingly paranoid about an Allied attack across the Channel. The Führer was already enraged at the presumption to leadership of a Free France based in London and North Africa by General Charles de Gaulle. Unable to strike at his foremost Gallic antagonist, the order instead came from Berlin to target members of de Gaulle's family, including his brother Jacques, by this point severely disabled as a result of suffering both encephalitis and Parkinson's disease. The Resistance had managed to hide the General's brother in a house in Grenoble, but, with the Gestapo circling, a journey to Switzerland became the only option.

Aware of the Abbé's expertise, Resistance leaders in Grenoble contacted him and, on the bitterly cold night of 9th November 1943, the clergyman managed to coordinate one of the most daring escapes of the entire Second World War. After removing the paralysed man from Grenoble under the cover of darkness, Abbé Pierre arranged for him to be hidden in the house of his colleague, the parish priest of Collonges-sous-Salève. From there, he was carried, at times by the Abbé himself, along one of the escape routes in the treacherous subalpine terrain that had been established over the course of the priest's previous mountain escapades to the relative safety of Geneva. Abbé Pierre had pulled off an astonishing coup, one that was to earn him the gratitude of General de Gaulle in future years and make his name among the forces fighting Fascism in France, a notoriety that would prove both a blessing and a curse.

By the start of 1944, Abbé Pierre was 'living rough' with his Maquis at Malleval near Lyon, helping to coordinate further assaults on German logistics and armaments. His health problems, however, returned to haunt him and, just before the end of January, he was persuaded to leave for more comfortable surroundings. A couple of days later, on 29th January, the Maquis was surrounded by German forces and, after a valiant fight, its members massacred. Abbé Pierre had no time to grieve the loss of his comrades, nor to reflect on how close his own brush with death had been. By the start of February, the Lyon Gestapo had identified his whereabouts and were preparing to pounce. As so often happened in the Abbé's life, a reprieve came in the nick of time.

The central information agency of the Resistance in Paris contacted an expert in heraldry and genealogy who had long acted as a double agent for them within the Vichy regime and asked him to help their agent out. His solution was to appoint the Abbé to investigate the Vichy Commissioner for Jewish Affairs, Louis Darquier de Pellepoix, a charlatan whose lies about his qualifications and pretensions to aristocratic ancestry had frustrated even the aged Marshal Pétain. With the seeming stamp of Vichy approval, Abbé Pierre set off nonchalantly to the Pyrenees, where it was hoped his mountaineering experience might help him in his real mission: to set up an escape route for Resistance fighters to Spain.

For all the hope placed in him by the Resistance, Abbé Pierre's time on the Spanish border proved to be short-lived. While the intelligence operation of the Free French was impressive, that of the Gestapo was even more so and, having only been in the south-west of France a few months, on 19th May 1944, he heard the unmistakable sound of boots on his staircase and a rifle butt banging on the door. He had been setting up contacts in Spain earlier that week, only to have his return tracked by the Nazis. 'My task is now ended,' he recalled saying to himself as the Gestapo burst in.

†

Whether it was by blessing, by luck, or by feat of derring-do, it is not possible to say, but, that very night, Abbé Pierre took advantage of Resistance-coordinated jailbreak and was free again. Helped by the robust anti-Fascist Bishop of Vitoria, he slipped over the border into neutral Spain and made contact with Allied forces via the Canadian Red Cross. He chose a new pseudonym, 'Abbot Houdin' – a nod to the performer Harry Houdini, whose reputation for near-impossible escapes the cleric was beginning to rival. Mindful of the need to avoid the Nazi agents operating in Spain with General Franco's blessing and who, along with the Gestapo in France, were baying for the clerical escapologist's blood, Abbé Pierre assumed yet another identity, that of Sir Harry Barlow, a downed RAF pilot, with papers giving him safe passage to join with British forces in Gibraltar. This he did and, from there, he made his way across the strait to the Free French forces in Algiers.

One might be forgiven for thinking that the good Abbé had had his fill of wartime adventures and perhaps was looking forward to a restful sojourn. But Pierre was not famed for his ability to sit still. Within a few days of arrival on 16th June 1944, he had recorded a message to the clergy of France, encouraging them to do all they could to support the invasion by the Allies on D-Day, just ten days prior to his arrival. The presumption of a part-priest, part-partisan in addressing the clergy of France did not go down especially well with the Papacy, not that the views of the Church hierarchy had ever been high up Abbé Pierre's list of priorities. One man it did impress was General de Gaulle, who, hearing that this was the same priest who had saved his brother's life, immediately invited the bedraggled cleric to dine with him at his residence in Algiers. Frustrated at being far from the action, Abbé Pierre requested a chaplaincy role with the forces returning to liberate France. This was granted and so Abbé Pierre journeyed to Casablanca, where he was enlisted as a chaplain in the Free French Navy.

Ironically, for a man who had begun the conflict in hospital bedclothes, Abbé Pierre ended the war in uniform, helping to liberate Paris. He was promoted well above his direct combat experience with the navy and, in January

1945, met with de Gaulle again, this time to receive the Croix de Guerre for his heroism. Abbé Pierre's mind, however, had already turned to the peace. Rather than share war stories with the General, as was expected, he proceeded to lecture him on the need for emergency food supplies to be redirected to Paris's civilian population. 'The Army of France has crossed the Rhine,' exploded de Gaulle in reply, 'and you come here to lecture me on baby milk!'

The breach in relations between soldier and priest was not, however, total. As peace loomed, de Gaulle sent another message to the Abbé, suggesting that, despite their very clear political differences, he ought to stand for election to the new parliament. This he did and in 1945 was elected an MP.

As the attentive reader will have noticed, Abbé Pierre was not one to rest on his laurels. After five years of representative politics, he decided to focus his attentions instead on charity work, where he felt he might make a more tangible difference. He began by buying an abandoned mansion in the wealthy Neuilly suburb of Paris, restoring it and inviting a number of homeless people to live in it with him. The first resident he invited in was an ex-convict who had to be fished out of the River Seine after an attempted suicide. Assisted by the redoubtable Lucie Coutaz, Abbé Pierre soon invited more homeless people to join him and so the first Emmaus community was born. Abbé Pierre's principle was simple: 'to serve the most needy first'. The charity now has over three hundred and thirty-six organisations in thirty-seven countries. Not a bad achievement for a failed monk.

Abbé Pierre finally died aged ninety-four in 2007. His later years were just as active as his earlier ones – from his

1954 hijacking of Radio Luxembourg to ask for donations of blankets for the poorest during France's coldest winter for years, to his decision to spend Christmas 1994 (when he was in his mid-eighties) squatting in a Parisian office building to highlight the plight of the homeless. He travelled around the world, meeting presidents, popes and potentates of every sort. His travel wasn't always smooth – he came through a plane crash in India and only survived a shipwreck off the coast of Uruguay by clinging to a plank of wood. Yet it was his heroism in the Second World War, his physical and mental courage and his implacable appetite for adventure that had first secured his place in the affections of the people of France. He was astonishingly well loved, even in later years when he would routinely bicker with other public figures and, perhaps not as mentally sharp as he had once been, he was conned into endorsing a book by a Holocaust denier (a particularly painful incident that, he confessed in his apology, brought back memories of his initial disbelief in that Lyon café in 1943). Despite this, he regularly topped any poll asking who was the 'most admired French person' (at least until, perplexed by fame, he wrote cease-and-desist letters, asking organisations to stop including his name).

Was it luck or blessing that broke him out of prison or brought him a last-minute reprieve, that steeled him on over the Alps with refugees on his back or kept him clinging to a plank as the sea tossed around him? Was it luck or blessing that gave him the courage of his convictions and let him stare the horrors of Nazism in the face? What distinguishes luck from blessing is, perhaps, a question best left to theologians. After all, Abbé Pierre was always happy to let others hammer out theory while he got on with practice. What we can say is that the life of the failed monk from Grenoble was a blessing to the nation of France in her darkest hour, to the Church in her trials and to many thousands of people who, in war and peace, owe their lives to him.

RESISTANCE IN THE CRADLES OF FASCISM

'First they came ...'

Germany

— CLEMENS AUGUST, BISHOP OF MÜNSTER AND GRAF VON GALEN —

The Lion of Münster

'**G**uns will make us powerful; butter will only make us fat!'

It was with these words that Hermann Göring tried to prepare the German people for the privations of the war that Nazism was about to unleash upon the world. It was an attempt to frame the Fascist struggle as a national one, requiring as much willpower on behalf of the housewife in the kitchen as the soldier at the front. Ironically, Göring himself, largely due to his own refusal to forswear rich food even at the height of wartime shortages, weighed in at eighteen and a half stone (118kg). Indeed, he was so corpulent that the American pilot who captured him had to request a more substantial plane to carry him, as the light aircraft originally tasked with the journey couldn't take his weight. But butter did, in fact, cause real trouble for the Nazis. Had it not been for butter, it is quite possible that Clemens von Galen would never have come to public prominence in quite the way he did.

Clemens August was the eleventh of thirteen children born to a devout Roman Catholic family in Westphalia in 1878, at the height of the Second German Empire. His parents made it their habit to attend Mass daily and were determined that their children would do so too. Clemens was not a thin child (indeed, he had a substantial waistline and a commanding height as an adult too, just about the only things he had in common with Göring). Knowing that he could also be stubborn, his parents decided that a very particular approach was needed in order to foster Catholic devotion in their antepenultimate child. When Clemens turned up late for morning worship, he would suffer the penalty of eating his morning collation without his favourite dairy product. The thought of going without butter was too much for young Clemens to bear and so he became a regular attendee of Mass, leading to a vocation to ordained ministry.

It was in this ministry that he was to find a role that led him to become 'The Lion of Münster' and, in his position as outspoken bishop of that city, draw the ire of the Nazi regime as well as the praise of resistance fighters, Jewish leaders and the Allied high command. Not that any of these necessarily affected him; it was no coincidence that, when he was made a bishop, he chose as his motto *Nec laudibus, nec timore,* meaning 'swayed by neither praise nor fear'. Having initially been written off as a tubby reactionary who owed his appointment to the fact that the Nazis thought he would make a pliable ally, he became a personal bête noire for the Führer and a symbol of resistance to Fascism, not least because his opposition to Nazism was not *in spite* of the fact that he was a German, but *because* of it. Butter may well have made Bishop von Galen fat, but he was a living witness in the very midst of Nazism that power is not only achieved by wielding a gun.

†

Other than the occasional threat of butterless breakfasts, Clemens August had, by all accounts, a happy childhood. The von Galen family were a fixture in the aristocratic circles of north-west Germany, where, in the small town of Dinklage, they had owned a castle since the mid-seventeenth century. Young Clemens enjoyed a youth punctuated by all the activities expected of his class at the time. He was sent to an elite Austrian boarding school run by the Jesuit order (where pupils were forbidden to speak any language other than Latin) and, when he returned home for holidays, spent long summers tromping around the countryside, hunting and fishing with his brother Franz. The family were not, however, out of touch with the rest of the world; his father was a Member of Parliament for the Centre Party, a political grouping that tried to steer a socially conscious middle course between left and right in the politically volatile climate of the newly united Germany. Clemens' brother Franz was to become the only Centre Party politician to oppose the Enabling Act that brought the Nazis to power (under the foolish premise that the Centre Party's leader, Franz von Papen, could exert a controlling influence on Hitler) and was sent to Sachsenhausen concentration camp for his trouble. The von Galen clan, therefore, gained a reputation as loyal public servants, but ones who could dig their heels in and cause difficulties if and when they so wished. This familial stubbornness was evident in Clemens too; one of his school reports contained the following sentences from an exasperated Jesuit: 'Infallibility is the main problem with Clemens, who under no circumstances will admit that he might be wrong. It is always the teacher who is mistaken.'

This single-mindedness was to be a defining feature of the bishop's life. Moving back to Germany to attend a less precocious secular public school in Lower Saxony wasn't enough to tempt the young Clemens to abandon his deeply held faith. When he graduated, he found that, in the yearbook presented to students as a leaving present, his entry read, 'Clemens doesn't chase girls or get drunk.' Even during the more strait-laced days of 1896, this was considered unusually chaste behaviour for an eighteen-year-old. He spent the next eight years immersed in study and, in 1904, was finally ordained a priest.

After a year or so working as a secretary for a clerical relative (there were von Galens dotted across Germany), he moved to become the priest of a deprived parish in Berlin, where his dominating figure and strong pastoral instinct won him a devoted following among the poor. Initially, von Galen focused exclusively on the immediate pastoral needs of those around him. Indeed, he had only two stated interests other than his parish work: pipe-smoking and listening to marching bands. His fellow clergy routinely commented on the spartan atmosphere of his rooms and the unpretentious nature of his dress, both attempts by the son of a Westphalian count to blend in with the gritty environment of Berlin.

Parish work ruled his life until the outbreak of the First World War, when he, in common with clergy across the western world, toed the line that it was a duty to fight for the fatherland. Defeat in 1918, therefore, represented the crumbling of the order that had been such an integral part of the worldview of von Galen's youth. He was appalled at the loss of the monarchy and, as political instability and food shortages devastated Berlin, he threw himself into social programmes and soup kitchens. These were projects he supported as much to prevent the ferment of revolutionary anti-clerical ideas (he had been horrified by reports of the mass slaughter of clergy in Russia after the revolution there) as to distract himself from a world now turned upside down. While von Galen's day-to-day work consisted of much the same practical help for the poorest as it had prior to the First World War, his political alignment shifted significantly to the right. He even went as far as to openly criticise the party his father and brother had served so assiduously, stating that it was far too left wing. The violent instability of interwar Germany only affirmed von Galen's reactionary opinions and, therefore, it was no surprise that, when he was announced as the new Bishop of Münster in 1933, local Nazis joined in the celebrations, even sending stormtroopers to his first service in a show of support.

Von Galen was a controversial choice as bishop. He only received the nomination after the favourite and a number of subsequent nominees turned down the offer of the role. Even then, the Vatican's chief diplomat in Germany, Cesare Orsenigo, tried to block the appointment, referring to von Galen as 'a bossy paternalist'. Ironically, it was Orsenigo who would later become close to the Nazis and von Galen who would turn his fire onto the Fascist government as tales of their crimes became known. Clemens August von Galen was nothing if not a man of surprises.

It took von Galen just under a month to fall foul of the governing party which had sent its armed goons to celebrate his enthronement; a turnaround which, even for a figure as combative and stubborn as the new Bishop of Münster, is pretty impressive. His first clash with the Nazis came over their efforts to shape schools around an entirely new curriculum, a move that serves as evidence of how Fascism sought to control the minutiae of public life, as well as how seriously it took the indoctrination of the young with a message of hate. Not long after von Galen's consecration on 28th October 1933, the Nazi superintendent of education for the Münster district ordered that all schools should teach their pupils about the fundamental inferiority of the Jewish race and warn them of the threat posed by 'the People of Israel' to the morale and structure of the German state. Bellicose as ever, von Galen refused to allow any change to the curriculum, immediately sending out precisely the opposite message to that intended by the Nazi reforms by composing a pastoral document to be read out in all churches and schools, emphasising the need to 'act with charity toward *all* men'.

Von Galen then went further, mocking the pseudo-religious ideological viewpoint of Nazi policy. One group, calling themselves *Deutsche Christen*, or 'The German Christians', tried to fuse Nazi anti-Semitism with the thought of the early Christian thinker Marcion of Sinope (despite the fact that all Churches had long since declared him a heretic) and demanded the removal from the Bible of both the Old Testament and any Jewish references in the New Testament (tricky given Jesus' birthplace, race, religion, etc.). Alongside these academically dubious figures stood a key guiding figure in German governmental religious policy at the time, a man known as the intellectual godfather of Nazism, Dr Alfred Rosenberg. Rosenberg was looking to eradicate Christianity in favour of a new Reich religion, based around a pseudo-pagan concept almost entirely of his own devising that he called 'Nordic Blood Soul'. Unsurprisingly, the combative von Galen found plenty to mock in these ideas. In an official response for a Catholic publication, he stated that such theories were worthy 'only of laughter in intellectual circles' and made a robust defence of the Hebrew scriptures and their absolutely essential role in both Christianity and Judaism. This public derision earned him the lifelong hatred of Rosenberg, who referred to the bishop as 'the greatest religious enemy of Nazi Germany' and later pushed for his execution. In the short term, his mockery also earned him a visit from high-ranking SS officer Jürgen Stroop. When Stroop told him in no uncertain terms that he must fall into line, Galen first mocked him for attending a Neo-Aryan Pagan service earlier that week, then suggested he ought to be more like his elderly mother, whom the bishop knew to be a devout Roman Catholic.

As the darkest sides of the Nazi regime became clearer and more public, von Galen was forced to move to riskier, more public action. In 1937, he made the journey to Rome and there helped compose a document on behalf of Pope Pius XI. Called *Mit Brennender Sorge* (With Burning Concern), it marked the high-water mark of official diplomatic pronouncements by the Papacy against the Nazis. In it, not only were the rights of the Church asserted but, with a clear sign of von Galen's hand, Nazi theories of race were strongly condemned, the role of Jewish culture and the Old Testament defended and, in a move that caused Hitler to fly into an explosive fit of rage, it not so subtly referred to the Führer as 'a prophet of nothingness … at whom Heaven laughs'. The document was smuggled back into Germany and distributed; the Nazi response was swift. Printing presses were seized, clergy arrested and imprisoned and laws against the Church tightened. It was a salutary lesson to von Galen about the ruthlessness of the regime and the risks that even minor resistance would bring with it. Privately conceding that the path he had chosen might well lead to his own execution, he steeled himself for what was to come.

†

The first person killed under the Nazi 'Aktion T4' involuntary euthanasia scheme was a disabled baby called Gerhard Kretschmar, injected with an overdose of barbiturates. Hitler personally signed the order to begin the killing of social undesirables (beginning with the mentally and physically disabled) in October 1939 but, tellingly, backdated it to a month earlier, although Gerhard had in fact been killed in July (as the first trial case in a scheme that eventually numbered about 300,000 people). The scheme began with children, whose parents were informed that they were being taken to centres where they could receive better care than they received either at home or in the existing network of nursing homes (which were almost entirely run by churches). After a couple of weeks, the parents would receive a letter informing them that their child had died of pneumonia or similar common conditions. In fact, they had been murdered by the Nazi state, designated as '*lebensunwertes Leben*' ('lives that are unworthy of life'). What began with disabled children soon progressed to adults, who by 1940 were being moved to specially built euthanasia centres and killed. The adults often proved more resistant than the children and so the Nazis began to experiment with the use of poison gas, enabling them to kill people from nursing homes, asylums and sanatoriums by the batch load as they arrived. It was a system that was to be repeated with grim efficiency after the Wannsee Conference of early 1942 when the Final Solution was set in motion.

While resistance was not immediate (the Nazi claim to be simply enacting administrative reorganisation was initially believed in a nation with a censored press), by late 1940 reports had begun to emerge of what was really happening at the sanatoriums. Von Galen and other bishops lobbied the Vatican to release a formal protest, restating that, by the laws of God and Man, 'the killing of an innocent person because of physical or mental defects is forbidden'. The protest fell on deaf ears, with one senior Nazi commenting, 'Thou shalt not kill is no commandment of God at all, but a Jewish invention.' Frustrated at progress through the official channels, and increasingly shocked by the stories that were brought to him day by day, by 1941 von Galen had decided that he needed to take the initiative himself.

In the summer of that year, he preached a series of sermons that were to result in the most widespread period of peaceful protest against the government during the whole of the Third Reich and the only one to result in an actual reversal (in public at least) of Nazi policy. It also resulted in von Galen being placed under effective house arrest, and those around him being imprisoned or killed. In his first sermon, he railed against abuses of rights, especially focusing on the tactics of the Gestapo and the climate of fear that they had created. He observed that no one was safe from their violations of freedom, from their prison cells and their concentration camps. At the end of the address, the enormous figure of the bishop leaned over the pulpit and bellowed, 'I, as a German, as a citizen, demand justice!'

The next week, he climbed into the pulpit again, a huge congregation having gathered, bringing together devout Christians, but also those committed to resistance, from secret Communists to Jews, attending undercover. It also attracted Nazi informers, Gestapo agents and party officials, all waiting for another attack on the regime that could be used against the bishop. They did not have to wait long. In his second sermon, von Galen moved from the evil deeds of the secret police to the injustice of the regime itself; it was not, he observed, Allied bombers who were destroying Germany (though the first raid to hit Münster had been a few weeks before, on 5th July, and, by the end of the war, nearly 90 per cent of the old city, including most of the cathedral, would be reduced to rubble). Rather, it was the poison and hatred that Fascism had sown from within.

Von Galen waited two weeks before preaching his third, final and most famous sermon. The summer light streamed through Münster Cathedral's hotchpotch of architecturally stylised windows – from narrow arched openings in the great Romanesque west front to the great pointed arches of the Von Galen chapels (named for a previous von Galen Prince-Bishop) – as the current bishop of that name climbed to his pulpit again and delivered a blistering attack. He decried the 'universal distrust' at the centre of the Nazi regime, as it forced neighbour to testify against neighbour, doctor to kill patient, German to denounce German. 'Woe on Germany,' he cried, 'woe to humanity itself!' His booming voice filling the rafters of the heaving cathedral, he announced to faithful and faithless alike that the Nazi regime was 'infected by Godlessness' and that their actions were so sinful that it would be better to resist and be executed than be complicit: 'Our motto must be Death rather than Sin.' He also revealed the actual details of the Aktion T4 programme. He told the story of a man receiving treatment for trauma in a sanatorium whose son was fighting on for the regime on the Eastern Front and of how that very same regime callously put to death the soldier's father as he was 'unproductive.' 'These are human beings, our brothers and sisters,' the bishop cried, 'productivity is no justification for killing.' He warned his audience that, if the Nazis could break the Ninth Commandment, 'Thou shalt not kill', they would be sure to break every other commandment as well.

The effect of the sermon was electrifying. Within days, thousands of copies had been circulated around Germany, despite immediate Gestapo attempts to suppress it. Copies reached soldiers at the front, many of whom wrote back to von Galen about the horrors they were experiencing there. Copies reached the University of Munich, where, inspired by the bishop's challenge, a group of young students led by Sophie Scholl formed 'The White Rose', a group dedicated to non-violent resistance to Nazism. Copies reached the underground Protestant seminary of Dietrich Bonhoeffer, who expressed his deep regard for the Roman Catholic bishop's stand. Copies even reached London, where the BBC began to broadcast them over their German service, in the hope of convincing the German population to reject Nazism. Copies also, of course, reached Nazi officials. Hitler was apoplectic and was said to be considering the suggestion of Martin Bormann (his secretary) and the pseudo-academic Rosenberg, von Galen's old nemesis, that the bishop should be hanged. Von Galen himself told his confidants that he had accepted what was about to come and was ready to die a martyr and so live out his exhortation to 'death rather than sin' in his own circumstances.

Bizarrely, it was Joseph Goebbels who saved von Galen. He had received numerous reports about rising opposition to the Aktion T4 programme, with stories of mobs storming government euthanasia centres in order to liberate loved ones, and was fearful that executing the respected cleric, who was now known as 'The Lion of Münster', would precipitate open rebellion, especially given the heavy casualties from the newly launched campaign on the Eastern Front. The Propaganda Minister convinced the Nazi leadership that executing the bishop immediately would be a mistake; 'in politics,' he said, 'one must know how to wait.' Hitler was eventually persuaded not to take action against 'that sly fox, Bishop von Galen', although he made a solemn vow that, when the Reich's supposedly inevitable victory came, retribution would be demanded from the bishop, and that he would pay with his life. In the meantime, the Führer called a halt to the public execution of the Aktion T4 programme (although it, of course, continued to operate with lower numbers and in secret). It was, arguably, the only successful domestic act of resistance within Germany during the Second World War.

While von Galen escaped execution, there was, naturally, retribution. He was placed under constant surveillance, his correspondence was checked and his movements were limited. The bishop's own sister, herself a nun, was imprisoned by the Gestapo and locked in a cellar to await a swift trial and probable execution, only to be rescued through a window and smuggled away into hiding. His brother was deported to a concentration camp, an ordeal he also managed to survive. Others were not so lucky, with the numbers of clergy and lay Church members (including the young resistance members of the White Rose) rounded up and executed by the regime rising sharply in the following months. Thirty-seven priests and members of religious orders were arbitrarily selected from the bishop's own diocese of Münster to enter concentration camps in von Galen's stead, with a third of them dying there.

This consequence of his outspokenness haunted von Galen for the rest of his life. At the end of the war, in recognition of his resistance, the Pope supposedly congratulated him on his bravery in the face of such barbarity, at which the newly minted cardinal replied that the truly brave ones were those who had been imprisoned and murdered for words and deeds that were not theirs but his: 'Many of my best priests died in concentration camps, and all because they distributed my sermons.' He was heartbroken by the arrests and executions, and, for the rest of his life, routinely questioned if resistance truly had been the best path. For his own part, he spent the rest of the war under effective house arrest. By the time Allied victory came in 1945, von Galen had endured captivity, the destruction of his cathedral in a bombing raid and the deaths of many of his family and friends. His health and spirit seemed broken but, as new problems began to arise in the rubble of a defeated nation, the lion stirred again.

As British, American and Soviet troops swept across Germany in 1945, tales of looting, murder and, especially, rape, against a predominately female civilian population began to be reported. Political or religious leaders with a shred of moral authority were few and far between in Germany at the time, but von Galen had now been liberated from the enforced silence that the Nazi regime had inflicted on him. A group of women appealed to him for justice. Fortified by his pipe and his brass band records, the von Galen of old awoke and took up the cause with gusto. He badgered Allied generals constantly to keep their troops in line, much to their chagrin, as they had expected to find a willing and pliable figurehead. Instead, they got a blistering response from von Galen, who informed the international press who had come to quote the influential words of the lion of German resistance that 'just as I fought against Nazi injustice, so will I fight any injustice, no matter where it comes from'. He set to work exactly as he had at the end of the First World War, visiting prisoners, setting up soup kitchens and finding hostels for those dispossessed by the violence.

At Christmas 1945, it was announced that von Galen, as a reward for his actions resisting the Nazis, would be made a cardinal in Rome. Despite attempts to prolong the turbulent prelate's house arrest and prevent the honouring of such an outspoken German figure, he made it to the Vatican and there announced that the achievement would stand as evidence that Germany could begin on a path of rehabilitation and return to 'the family of nations'. He returned to Münster and, outside the bombed-out ruins of his cathedral, addressed the city, making sure to thank those in the resistance and in the ordinary ranks of the clergy who had made his own resistance possible. A couple of days later, the Lion of Münster was dead. Lack of medical supplies and facilities in a desolate city meant that a perforated appendix went undiagnosed and became fatal. He never got to see the new Germany free from the twin horrors of Communist and Fascist totalitarianism, for which he so dearly longed. And so, the city, and the nation, mourned its lion; a man who, be it for love of nation, love of humanity, love of God, or just love of butter, always sought to stand up for the weak and poor and to serve justice as he saw it.

Could von Galen have done more? Should he even have done what he did? Was he a selfish reactionary, looking out for the interests of the Church alone? Did he even, at times, exhibit some of the deep-rooted anti-Semitism of his class that made it easier for Nazism to take root in Germany? The answer may well be yes, although not, it must be said, an unqualified, absolute 'yes', to each of these questions. In the twenty-first century, we demand our public figures to be perfectly good or perfectly evil. Bishop von Galen was at neither extreme – he was a complex and imperfect figure, rooted in the attitudes of a particular time and place. And yet, regardless of his motives or the scale of his rebellion against Nazism, such were the horrors of that time and place, the absolute lack of hope, that von Galen's acts of resistance, small though they were, must be counted. He bears witness, better than any other in this collection, to the power of the symbolic act and the ability of words to provide a focal point for resistance as much as any action. He may not have directly saved as many lives as others, but his words exerted such power that he forced even the supposedly unstoppable force of the Thousand-Year Reich to change its plans. He may not have blown up bridges or freed prisoners, but his charisma inspired those, from Bonhoeffer to the White Rose, who sought to keep a flame alive in Germany's darkest days. He may not have died alongside those who perished in the concentration camps, but the power of his witness clearly made its mark even among those who survived them. Perhaps his most remarkable epitaph came from the regional association of Jewish communities, who made a public statement of mourning on the bishop's death. The German Jewish population had fallen from half a million in 1933, when von Galen began his resistance, to just over thirty thousand by the time he died; if anyone knew the failings of internal German resistance, it was them. And yet they honoured von Galen thus: 'he was one of the few upright and conscientious men who fought against racism in a most difficult time. We shall always honour the memory of the deceased bishop.'

— DIETRICH BONHOEFFER —

Thinker, Fighter, Pastor, Spy

Dietrich Bonhoeffer was hard as nails. Physically imposing, intellectually sharp and incredibly charming, he was a double agent, a smuggler of refugees and a would-be assassin. He was also an ordained minister in the Lutheran-Reformed Church. Even had the rise of Fascism and the ensuing world war not intervened, it is very probable that Bonhoeffer would be remembered as one of the great theological minds of the twentieth century. However, his was to be a life shaped not just by books but by bombs and bullets too. His is in many ways a swashbuckling tale, one that takes in all sorts of places and people, from the dreaming spires of Oxford to the mean streets of Harlem, from caring for the street kids of interwar Berlin to trying to kill the Führer himself.

In many ways, Bonhoeffer's tale is a tragedy. He failed in his attempts to convince the majority of his Church to actively oppose Nazism, he failed in his plot to kill Hitler and, ultimately, he failed to save his own life. And yet Bonhoeffer's story tells us something crucial about Christian resistance to Fascism: in the Gospel according to St John it says, 'He that loveth his life shall lose it; and he that hateth his life shall keep it unto life eternal.' Success or failure, therefore, is not measured in terms of achieving goals or even avoiding death, but by clinging to the idea of the life, and the love, that is eternal. Bonhoeffer's resistance was crucial in that he kept that flame alive, even though acting on it led him to the scaffold. Dietrich Bonhoeffer's steeliness came not from a robust confidence in his own abilities, or charm, or attractiveness, but from a faith in the idea that love would conquer death, and that his own life counted as nothing. As he was led out to execution, a Nazi prison camp doctor (not a breed renowned for their emotional observations) commented on how, in his whole grim career of sending people to their deaths, he had never seen anyone approach the scaffold as bravely as Bonhoeffer. The sight of this bravery deeply perturbed him, unable as he was to comprehend it. Bonhoeffer lived a life that made Nazis quake with rage and he died a death that made them quake with fear.

His father was a pre-eminent psychiatrist at the psychiatric medicine unit at the University of Breslau. Despite Bonhoeffer senior being a famous opponent of the ideas of Sigmund Freud, it was pretty clear from the sizeable brood of children he and his wife produced that this opposition didn't extend to an absolute rejection of the sexual. Dietrich was one of eight children and was born a twin. In a family of pragmatic and scientific thinkers, he was always marked out for his deep interests in philosophy, metaphysics and, of course, religion. Many years after his death, Bonhoeffer's younger sister would reminisce about when she and Dietrich's twin sister were moved out of their communal nursery to a new room separate to Dietrich. He informed the sisters that he could hear them chattering each evening after praying and so, considerate elder brother that he was, offered to 'rap on the wall three times' to remind them to 'think about the dear Lord'.

In 1912, when Dietrich was just six years old, his father took up the post of senior psychiatry professor at the University of Berlin. The move to the capital threw the family into the social and intellectual elite of the German Empire. While his father was agnostic, his mother was a woman of faith and ensured that holidays such as Christmas and Easter were celebrated accordingly. However, Bonhoeffer's parents were primarily concerned with giving their children the broadest intellectual grounding possible and would read them academic tracts alongside Bible stories and nursery tales. The children would routinely be called to discussions round the dinner table with some of the pre-eminent scientists and philosophers of the day. All this undoubtedly made for an intellectually engaged childhood, but, it seems, a happy one.

Having waited out the majority of the First World War, the Bonhoeffers tried to use their connections to prevent Dietrich's elder brother, Walter, from being called up at all. But by 1918 they could put it off no longer, and Walter was sent off to France to fight for the Kaiser. Just two weeks later, he was dead, riddled with shrapnel in the horrific mire of the Western Front. As he lay dying of his wounds, he found time to pen a final letter to his family, begging them not to worry. The family was wracked with grief. Dietrich, now twelve, was given his brother's Bible and, always a child of faith, began to take his beliefs much more seriously, drawing on a strength that eluded his heartbroken parents. It was still a surprise, however, when, after passing his exams at secondary school, Dietrich announced his desire to be a pastor. His intellectual capacity was clear, even as an adolescent, and it was naturally assumed that he would follow his father into a career in psychiatry or, at a push, his surviving brother into the legal profession. But with a stubborn sense of his own calling that was to become a hallmark of his life and death, Dietrich was adamant: he wanted to study theology and he wanted to be ordained. This he did, racing through bachelors, masters and doctoral degrees at the University of Berlin before he was twenty-three.

The German Evangelical Church (a union of Lutheran and Calvinist denominations that represented the mainstream of German Protestantism) knew they had a bright (possibly dangerously so) young man on their hands. Proclaiming that he was too young to be made a minister, but wanting to stretch him just a little further to test his mettle, the Church arranged in 1928 to send him on a series of placements around the world. It began with a job assisting the German-speaking congregation in Barcelona. Here, following the line of almost all his fellow pastors at the time, his sermons and lectures expressed a tacit approval of nationalism (especially as a bulwark against Communism, the horrors of which were becoming clear in the USSR). Overall, however, his time in Spain was to foster little more than a lifelong fascination with the mechanics of bullfighting. He briefly returned to Germany to submit a dissertation and sort out his next trip abroad. What was to follow was a whirlwind of road trips, revelation and (in his own words) 'rapturous passion', that was to change the direction of Bonhoeffer's life forever.

In the summer of 1930, among the mass of different languages, garbs and skin tones that composed those queuing up to get their papers checked at the Ellis Island immigration station in Upper New York Bay stood the unmistakable tall, blond figure of Dietrich Bonhoeffer. His primary focus in New York was supposed to be a consolidation of his academic reputation, lecturing at the prestigious Union Theological Seminary, where the East Coast's white, liberal, Protestant establishment taught polite platitudes to its potential pastors. It did not take long for Bonhoeffer to express frustration at his surroundings. 'In New York,' he wrote, 'they preach about everything; the only thing they do not mention is the Gospel of Jesus Christ.' Increasingly morose and sceptical during the winter months, Bonhoeffer headed south on a road trip that December, ending up in Cuba, where he indulged his predilection for a good cigar. (It was a love he would carry with him all his life, once declaring that a particular cigar – a gift from the theologian Karl Barth – was so good that it made him question 'the probabilities of reality'.) His route took him through the Southern states of the USA at the very height of the Jim Crow laws. What he saw shocked him deeply. He wrote letters home decrying the treatment of black people as 'shameful' and 'repugnant'. The trip prompted a development in his interest in black theology as, he said, it was from a black preacher alone that he had heard the 'genuine proclamation of the gospel in America'. On his return to New York, he set about deepening his relationship with another outsider in the great Protestant broiling pan that was the Union Seminary – namely one of the few black students, Albert Franklin Fisher, who, in turn, persuaded Bonhoeffer to deepen his relationship with one of New York City's most prominent black churches.

Quite what the congregation of the Abyssinian Baptist Church, West 138th Street, Harlem, thought of the tall, dapper German who appeared in their midst one day is not recorded. It is said that, even today, eleven o'clock on a

Sunday morning remains the most segregated time in the United States. Bonhoeffer threw himself into the community there, leading Sunday schools, taking part in worship and even preaching, though the congregation were more used to the exuberant hallelujahs of the great minister Adam Clayton Powell than the notoriously analytical and close textual style of the bespectacled German.

Bonhoeffer had been changed, even if his preaching style remained somewhat more rigid than that of his black counterparts. In his own words, Christianity had moved from 'phraseology to reality'. When his Easter break came, Bonhoeffer planned another road trip, setting out with a Frenchman named Jean Lasserre (who would spend the Second World War hiding a British wireless transmitter in his bedroom, in the style of René from *'Allo 'Allo*, and who later became a sort of travel agent for international pro-peace speakers). The two Europeans travelled the length and breadth of America, even making a foray into Mexico. Where possible, Bonhoeffer insisted that they stop and worship in black churches, deepening his conviction that a lived-out, active faith was needed to replace the dry academia he had known in Germany.

Yet it was back to Germany that Bonhoeffer was called, and so, in 1931, he was finally made a minister in the Church of the Evangelical Union. Now a pastor in Berlin, he insisted on taking a class of the naughtiest boys – against the advice of the elderly volunteer who had the pleasure of teaching them at the time. The classroom was at the top of the building and, as the Prussian pensioner led the single-minded young minister up the stairs, they were met by a hail of books, pencils and board erasers from the assembled catechumens above. Reaching the relative safety of the mezzanine floor, the elder man made his apologies and darted back down to safety. Bonhoeffer, however, continued up the stairs. Once there, he told the gathered prepubescent malcontents that he wished simply to tell them a story. If they behaved, he would tell them more the following week; if not, he wouldn't. It doesn't technically qualify as a miracle, but the following week when he arrived, he was met not with a hail of books but a quiet, rapt audience waiting for the second instalment of the Gospel narrative. The analytic, Teutonic caterpillar of old had become a passionate, spellbinding butterfly.

Soon, however, Bonhoeffer was to come across challenges much greater than recalcitrant schoolboys. On 30th January 1933, Adolf Hitler finally became Chancellor of Germany after a period of intense political wrangling. Just two days later, Bonhoeffer took to the airwaves, warning in a radio broadcast that the man his party called Führer was, in fact, a *Verführer*, a seducer, sent to lead the German people astray. Bonhoeffer's astonishing diatribe was taken off the air while he was still mid-flow.

Aware of the potential power of the state Protestant Churches, Hitler called and subsequently rigged elections to key Church positions in July of that year. Bonhoeffer rallied behind pastor Martin Niemöller who opposed the so-called *Deutsche Christen* faction, which sought to include statements about the superiority of the Aryan race in the Creed and remove the Old Testament from the Bible altogether. The campaign against the Nazification of the Lutheran Church was a failure, partly, as Bonhoeffer himself saw it, because there had been too many attempts at compromise to win over those who saw Hitler as a bulwark against Communism. Niemöller later reflected on the capitulation of the German intellectual and religious establishments in the face of Nazism with the following poem, written after his release from Dachau concentration camp in 1945:

First they came for the socialists, and I did not speak out –
because I was not a socialist.
Then they came for the trade unionists, and I did not speak
out –
because I was not a trade unionist.
Then they came for the Jews, and I did not speak out –
because I was not a Jew.
Then they came for me – and there was no one left to
speak for me.

Dietrich Bonhoeffer became determined that he *would* speak out – even if his own Church body would not. He, Niemöller and others formed the Confessing Church, splitting from the now Nazi-controlled Evangelical Church with the stated aim of opposing the government. Unable to take any official post under the new regime, Bonhoeffer was on the move again and, in late 1933, accepted a post to minister to a small German congregation in the glamorous surroundings of Sydenham, south London. He faced enormous criticism from his colleagues, including Karl Barth, for 'abandoning the house of the Church while it is on fire'. The insult stung and Bonhoeffer's time in London was comparatively brief. It was not, however, without its benefits: his new contacts would prove crucial when he became a spy.

It was a cold Pomeranian evening and, in the hall of an ancient Prussian estate about seventy miles from Gdansk, a group of pale would-be pastors was gathered around the piano, singing the African American spiritual 'Go down Moses' with a lustiness that only several large lagers can bring. Their circumstances were even more astonishing than their choice of music – they were in Pomerania as part of a 'seminary on the run' training for ministry despite the explicit order of Himmler against the enterprise. Bonhoeffer was seated at the piano, playing the spiritual with a dramatic, even melodramatic, flair that would not have been out of place in the praise bands of New Orleans. Bonhoeffer had returned to Germany in 1935 (despite being sorely tempted by an offer from Gandhi to study under him in India) and had begun an underground theological college to train up ministers who could resist the Nazification of Christianity in Germany. Barth had been forced into exile in neutral Switzerland in 1935 and Niemöller was under the constant watch of the Gestapo, culminating in his incarceration in Sachsenhausen in 1938, leaving Bonhoeffer, at the age of just thirty, de facto head of the largest Christian body dedicated to resistance in Nazi Germany. The training of ministers for the Confessing Church had been illegal since the summer of 1937, and Bonhoeffer's own teaching licence had been indefinitely suspended since August 1936, and so, behind the masks of smoke, drink and song, there was a genuine fear, a risk of betrayal and arrest, and of ending up in one of the concentration camps whispered about behind closed doors. Yet by the winter of 1938/9, Bonhoeffer was moving towards a more explicit position in his desire to oppose the Nazis, one that pushed him to engage in activities much more dangerous than even the underground seminary, one that was ultimately to cost him his life.

In early 1938, he got in touch with contacts from his days in Berlin high society at the Military Intelligence Bureau, known as the Abwehr. The Abwehr had become the centre of anti-Nazi activity within the German military establishment. Staff there passed information to the British and others and helped Jews and those threatened by Nazi policies to escape to safety. Through his Abwehr contacts, Bonhoeffer became aware of the Nazi plan to unleash 'total war' upon Europe. He soon realised that, despite the fact he was now banned from any public position or even from entering the German capital, his call-up papers would be processed with particular care and attention by the Gestapo. Utterly unable to swear an oath to Hitler, he returned to America. And there he might have stayed, but, aware of the theology of action he had developed, his own conscience began to niggle at him. A couple of months after his arrival, war was declared in Europe and Bonhoeffer made the fateful decision to get back on the last scheduled steamer to Germany. On arrival, he joined the Abwehr, ostensibly so that they could use his wide international contacts in the war effort. In fact, the bespectacled clergyman had swapped theology for espionage and was now a double agent, actively seeking to bring down the Nazi regime from the inside.

Already used to smuggling seminarians across the forests of East Prussia, Bonhoeffer now put the contacts made abroad to good use and helped smuggle a number of people out of the country. This mostly consisted of arranging the contacts to help Jews escape across the mountains into neutral Switzerland, but also included arranging the flight of his twin sister Sabine and her Jewish husband, whom he managed to get to London, despite the perils of war and blockade, in 1940. His time in England had earned him the friendship of the Anglican Bishop of Chichester, whom Bonhoeffer used as a conduit to try and pass Abwehr information to the British government. His intricate knowledge of the forests and boltholes of the East Prussian wilderness from his days running the seminary enabled him to arrange the delivery of supplies as well as potential escape routes for resistance movements seeking to sabotage Nazi operations there. Unlikely though the joint role of clergyman and spy might already seem to be, it is difficult to emphasise just how much Bonhoeffer would have been seen as going against the grain of what it meant to be a German Christian at the time. The Nazis and their plants in the mainstream Protestant churches were using the theology of turning the other cheek, of submission and sacrificial obedience to cajole the vast majority of German Christians into either active or tacit support of the government. Bonhoeffer, by contrast, viewed the constant frustration of the Nazis as a mission from God: 'The defeat of our nation,' he wrote, 'is necessary for Christian civilisation to survive.'

Bonhoeffer's role in smuggling Jews to Switzerland could not last long. The Gestapo was already incredibly suspicious of the Abwehr's claims that this man who had denounced Nazism from the very beginning could be of any use to the war effort. Indeed, his Gestapo file read that he was 'totally in opposition' to the regime. Initially, Himmler's secret police decided to investigate his frequent trips to the Swiss border in terms of fraud – the idea of a corrupt cleric making money from people smuggling would have made a great propaganda victory. Consequently, Bonhoeffer was arrested in April 1943, just a few months after he had become engaged to his long-term friend and associate Ruth von Kleist-Retzow. He was kept in the infamous Tegel prison, where his fiancée managed to smuggle him food and letters, enabling him to keep up his contacts and, as if things had gone full circle, return to some theological writing in his correspondence. The great theological work of Bonhoeffer's, still in print and read across the world today, had already been written in 1937. Entitled *The Cost of Discipleship*, after just over a year in prison, Dietrich Bonhoeffer was about to discover exactly how costly his discipleship was.

†

On 20th July 1944, a suitcase was smuggled into the operations room of Hitler's 'Wolf's Lair' headquarters in East Prussia. It was a warm day and so the Führer ordered that his situation conference about the progress of the war (now being fought on two protracted fronts) should take place with his military staff in the main room of the complex, as opposed to his reinforced bunker. The handsome aristocrat Colonel Claus von Stauffenberg was the only man in the room who knew exactly what was in the suitcase, namely a bomb, designed to kill Hitler and precipitate a mass mutiny of the German army leading to a *coup d'état*, known as Operation Valkyrie. At 12.40, von Stauffenberg left to take a telephone call. Two minutes later, the bomb exploded, killing four people. Unfortunately for the conspirators – and for Dietrich Bonhoeffer – Adolf Hitler was not among them. Hitler lost hearing in one ear and his trousers, which were blown to shreds by the blast, but not his life.

His revenge was brutal. The plot had been hatched and executed with the full support of the Abwehr, the culmination of the efforts of a circle of resistance agents in the organisation, including Dietrich, his brother and his brother-in-law. The conspirators weren't stupid, and the extent of the plot took some time to unfold. However, by September 1944, the Gestapo had finally found documents incriminating Dietrich, and, after continued harsh treatment in Tegel, in February 1945 they moved him to concentration camps (first Buchenwald and finally Flossenbürg) to await his fate. It is testament to Abwehr ingenuity that it was only in early April 1945 (not even a month before Hitler's own demise) that the full extent of the plot became known. In the frenzy of the collapsing Nazi state, the home of the Abwehr's ultimate head, Admiral Canaris, was ransacked, his diaries found and the scale of the organisation's (and Bonhoeffer's) efforts against the Nazis was revealed. Hitler flew into a rage and, with the Allies closing in on Berlin, ordered one last liquidation of prisoners.

On Sunday 8th April 1945, Dietrich Bonhoeffer had just said a service for his fellow prisoners, as had been his custom during his whole time in the concentration camp. As he finished his prayers, a group of soldiers arrived to drag him away to a hastily convened show trial masquerading as a court martial. Bonhoeffer calmly turned to a British prisoner who had been worshipping with him and asked him to pass a simple message on to his old friend Bishop Bell of Chichester: 'For me this is the beginning of life.' He said not a single word in his defence when he was dragged before the SS judge but quietly accepted his fate. The following morning, he was led out to a hastily constructed gallows and stripped. Before being executed, he knelt quietly to pray and commended his soul to God. Then they hanged him with piano wire. The prison camp doctor, watching the events from behind a shed on the other side of the yard, said he had, in nearly a half century as a doctor, 'never seen anyone die so submissive to the will of God'. Dietrich Bonhoeffer was hard as nails.

ITALY

— DON PIETRO PAPPAGALLO —

The Forger-Priest of the Esquiline Hill

'The history of the saints is predominately the history of insane people.' So Italian dictator and founder of European Fascism Benito Mussolini is supposed to have commented when asked about his views on Christianity. Undoubtedly, many of those called to a holy life have been manifestly foolish in the mould of St Simeon the Holy Fool. Simeon was a sixth-century Christian figure who was imbued with a childish simplicity and became famous for his erratic acts: he kept a dead dog as a pet and went around the city of Edessa throwing nuts at church-goers and anointing the sick with mustard, all the while subsisting on a diet of beans, which had exactly the effect on his digestion that you would expect. Perhaps unsurprisingly, such behaviour earned Simeon the epithet 'The Fool'.

The question, however, of what actually constitutes folly is a complex one – indeed, the Bible itself dedicates much of the Book of Proverbs to working it out. There are perhaps degrees of foolishness between the extremes of an office job and dragging a dead dog around. Yet, very often, the line between foolishness and bravery is considerably more blurry than in the case of St Simeon. Are injudicious, death-or-glory types of valiant and self-sacrificial behaviour saintly or stupid? Putting one's neck on the line, even for a seemingly doomed cause, is often part and parcel of saintliness. Indeed, the unsuccessful resolution of such efforts is a precondition of the crown of the martyr. Are those who commit such acts inspired or, as Mussolini clearly thought, insane?

One such example is of a man initially thought to be a bit simple but whose bravery led him to deceive the bureaucracy of the Nazis and save hundreds of lives. It was a bravery that led, also, to his betrayal and execution by the very regime he had hoodwinked so successfully. The man in question was the Italian resistance hero Don Pietro Pappagallo; which, translated into English, would be 'the Reverend Peter Parrot'.

While not quite on the level of St Simeon, the chubby chaplain to a community of nuns hardly cuts the figure of your average resistance hero. Don Pietro certainly didn't look like the bedraggled and foolish saints of old. Far from striking a gaunt and waiflike figure and subsisting on locusts and wild honey, he was something of a bon viveur. From the rich and creamy burrata of his native Puglia to the little cornetto pastries he would devour with his daily coffee, Don Pietro liked his food. The photographs that exist of him reveal that his not inconsiderable appetite took its toll, with his cincture and cassock barely holding in his sizeable gut. But if Don Pietro was big-bellied, he was even bigger hearted. His very Italian love of food was matched only by his very Italian hospitality. The city of Rome is filled with great, closed Baroque doorways, behind which her clergy live in gilded but isolated splendour. But Don Pietro Pappagallo was neither haughty prince of the Church nor saintly ascetic hermit (realistically, living on top of a pillar would have been both contrary to his naturally sociable nature and a logistical impossibility given his proportions). His table was an open one where he would break bread (accompanied, of course, by great quantities of olive oil and butter) with priests and prostitutes, sisters and soldiers, Communists and Carmelites. A bubbling generosity was hard-wired into his character even to the very end, giving blessing to all those – Jews, Protestants, atheists and those in between – who found themselves meeting their maker alongside him in the smoky gloom of the Ardeatine Caves.

As unlikely as he may have appeared, Pietro Pappagallo exhibited exactly the commitment to ideals that had led to the martyrdom of many saints before. Indeed, it was his casual attitude to his own safety that made it so easy to betray him. Furthermore, to us, with the benefit of hindsight, his strategy of helping everyone who came to his door, in a city awash with spies and double agents, might seem so foolish as to be practically suicidal. Whether Don Pietro Pappagallo really was mad to do what he did is for you, dear reader, to decide. But even if he was, it might just be a sign of his saint-liness – brave and foolish in equal measure, as that quality so often proves to be.

In Shakespeare's *Twelfth Night*, set in the Adriatic coastal region of Illyria, the pompous Malvolio famously says, 'some are born great, some achieve greatness, and some have greatness thrust upon them'. If Pietro Pappagallo was great, it was certainly not down to his modest birth on the opposite shore of the Adriatic, in the tiny town of Terlizzi, near Bari, in June 1888.

Terlizzi was not a particularly auspicious place to enter the world. The town was notorious for its unhealthiness and poverty, even by the standards of late nineteenth-century southern Italy. It was also noted for its biblical plagues of locusts in the summer months, rendering agriculture, good health or going outdoors practically impossible. Pietro was the fifth child of eight born to Pasquale and Maria Tommasa Pappagallo. He was an artisan engaged in the rope-making business; she a devout, somewhat domineering housewife. It was Pietro's devoted *mamma* who first decided that he might have a vocation to the ministry while he was working as an apprentice in his father's workshop. Through scrimping, saving and selling off some property that the family had acquired, she managed, by the time Pietro was in his teens, to amass enough funding to have Pietro educated for the priesthood.

Pietro was not an especially accomplished student, but the Church was forgiving and Pietro was made a deacon in February 1914. The world that Pietro had grown up in was one marked by familiarities: the ancient trade of his father dependent on a regional economy unchanged since Roman times; the devout faith of his mother, with its prayers and patterns of worship unshaken since the Council of Trent; the political sureties of crown, people and altar that shaped the lives of most Europeans. That certainty was about to be cast aside forever in favour of the brave new world of the twentieth century. The murder of an Austrian Archduke must have seemed as remote to the newly ordained deacon in southern Italy as it doubtless did to the peasant farmers of rural France or the Bright Young Things of the London season, as remote even as it must have seemed to an out-of-work Viennese painter roughing it in Munich. Yet the war unleashed by Franz Ferdinand's assassination utterly changed the course of these and millions of other lives; indeed, the trigger that was pulled in Sarajevo caused not only the deaths of the Austrian heir and his wife, but, in the two world wars that followed it, millions more as well.

Italy was a somewhat reluctant participant in the First World War. Initially thought to be on the side of the Central Powers, the opportunity to get one over on its old foe Austria–Hungary proved too tempting and so, on 3rd May 1915, Italy revoked its old alliance and, twenty days later, declared war against Austria–Hungary. The war was popular among all classes except the clergy. Pope Benedict XV, a bespectacled and bookish Genoese aristocrat, ordered a policy of neutrality on the part of the Church, presciently decrying the war as 'the suicide of civilised Europe'. At the start of the conflict, he published a prayer imploring the intercession of Christ, who 'felt deep compassion for human misfortunes' and was 'the Prince of Peace', to end the conflict. It was this prayer that Pietro Pappagallo distributed among the congregation on Easter Sunday 1915, when he celebrated Mass for the first time, having been ordained a priest the day before. This call to compassion affected Pappagallo deeply.

He was soon sent to be an assistant teacher at a Church-run boarding school not far from his home town, a job that could hardly be considered a plum position. He remained in this less than glamorous role for ten years. However, his quiet, dogged pastoral ministry eventually made a mark somewhere, as, in 1925, at the age of thirty-seven, Pappagallo finally received something akin to a promotion. He was sent to further his study of canon law not up the road to the sleepy metropolis of Bari, but to the great pulsating hub of Rome.

The Eternal City was simultaneously the heart of global Catholicism and the capital of the adolescent Italian state; the exact status of the city, and the relative jurisdictions (both legal and moral) of the two competing authorities, had never really been resolved since the capture of Rome from the forces of Pope Pius IX by Garibaldi in 1871. As such, an uneasy tension reigned, with successive popes refusing to set foot on Italian soil, rendering them 'prisoners of the Vatican'. Indeed, it was only in 1918 that the Vatican formally reversed its infamous *Non Expedit* decree which had banned Roman Catholics (who constituted about 95 per cent of the Italian population) from voting or participating in democratic politics in the newly united Italian nation. Realistically, as with Papal pronouncements on issues as diverse as the consumption of wine during Lent and contraception, many Roman Catholics merrily ignored the official doctrinal adjunction. However, large numbers toed the line and so Italian politics became markedly secular in its nature, lacking a coherent Christian Democratic Party (as existed in other European states) and with far left and far right wielding disproportionate influence. If the Papacy had hoped to wield some influence in Italian democratic politics, the lifting of the ban in 1918 was too little, too late. In the heady post-war atmosphere, a single figure pushed himself to the forefront of Italian politics and, in 1922, he marched on Rome, demanding that the diminutive and vacillating King Vittorio Emanuele III make him Prime Minister. The monarch, who had spent most of his reign following his father's advice that all the knowledge a king required was an ability to 'sign his name, read a newspaper, and mount a horse', gave in to Mussolini's demands and made the man who called himself 'Il Duce' (a title he borrowed from the one-eyed poet turned adventurer Gabriele D'Annunzio who had launched a short-lived city state in the Croatian coastal city of Fiume) the de facto ruler of Italy.

Mussolini had begun life as a committed socialist and a key part of his appeal to ordinary Italians was his claim that

Italy was a proletarian nation locked in a struggle against plutocratic forces (in particular, Britain) who sought to constrain her economic development – an easily believable lie for the millions that made up the Italian working underclass. He was also an ardent opponent of religion, in particular Catholicism. Realising that Mussolini's populist secularism was beginning to hold sway with large parts of the working class, the Roman Catholic Church began to send clergy out specifically to partake in industrial mission. One such cleric was Pietro Pappagallo, who, in 1927, left his studies and found himself helping to run a hostel.

It had been set up for workers at the enormous Rome textile plant of the chemical giant SNIA SpA, situated on the Via Prenestina, to this day a grim industrial district at the back of the Termini station, a far cry from the pavilions and palaces for which Rome is best known, which made the ropery of Terlizzi look idyllic by comparison. The conditions in the hostels were appalling. The work, too, was incredibly dangerous, with almost all workers exposed to harmful chemicals. Medical care for the resulting sicknesses was non-existent and, consequently, many found their lungs filling up with bubbling fluid, leading to a death as horrific as any on the Western Front. In this abyss of human existence, the workers headed into a downward spiral, seeking pleasures where they could find them: a flurry of sexual encounters, consensual or otherwise, with prostitutes or each other; pay spent on vast amounts of tobacco and, of course, drink. Crucially, the company could demand unlimited overtime and sacked anyone who lagged behind, as well as paying their Roman workers a fraction of what they paid in their primary factory in Milan. What Pappagallo saw shocked him and, for the first time in his life, aged nearly forty, he decided to stick his head above the parapet.

Pappagallo wrote to the Vatican secretariat on workers' affairs, detailing the abuses he saw and commenting, 'I do not find all of this just'. Doubtless aware of the Fascist rhetoric of a need for all classes to struggle in order to attain greater glory for the Italian fatherland, Pappagallo included these lines: 'I cannot be brought round by arguments about political convenience, that indeed don't interest me at all.'

There Pappagallo might have stayed; a workhorse slum priest, faithfully ministering in the slough of despond that was Rome's industrial underbelly. Instead, with Vatican insiders determined to come to an arrangement with Mussolini's new regime, it was considered that the would-be worker priest was too troublesome to be involved in industrial relations and so, after barely a year in the post, Pappagallo was sacked. Little did those insiders know just how much more trouble the plump padre had in him.

†

Dismissal from the factory might have been the end for Pietro Pappagallo but, in fact, it was only the beginning. Despite opposition from the grey suits at the Vatican (every profession has its jobsworths), his bishop pleaded his cause and so, in 1928, Pappagallo was given a role at the very bottom of the food chain (he was, specifically, in charge of dunking the long line of children brought for baptism) at the great Papal Basilica of St John Lateran. That position, too, was to be short-lived. Pappagallo had made a reputation as something of a loose canon and, after barely a year in the job, he was informed again that his services were no longer needed. Pappagallo became desperate; a return to the stultifying atmosphere of southern Italy was a serious possibility and, while his affection for his siblings back in his home town remained strong, he felt a powerful calling to remain in Rome. Perhaps he sensed it was there that he'd finally make a difference. Perhaps he just didn't want to make rope. However, if he could not find a position – ideally one that required minimal input from the Vatican diplomats who had taken against him – then a one-way ticket home to Terlizzi was inevitable.

The order of the Oblate Sisters of the Holy Child Jesus were an odd bunch. In the poky Roman town house that served as their convent, they lived a life dedicated to the principles of a spiritual childhood, taking joy in the simple things. They were not, properly speaking, really nuns at all, but, rather, 'oblate sisters' – lay women dedicated to the education and religious instruction of girls and young women. The order had originally been founded by Anna Moroni, a seventeenth-century washerwoman who found herself too attractive to serve as a domestic servant (the men of Rome were not famed for marital fidelity even then). Faced with prostitution, she turned to the Church and, under the auspices of educating other would-be prostitutes, set up a lay order of women dedicated to education and simplicity of life. Each of its communities had a house with a place of worship attached, where otherwise redundant clergy often found gainful employment offering spiritual guidance and religious services to the women. The community in Rome had a house on the Via Urbana, a thoroughfare on the Esquiline Hill, a maze of sleepy streets still dominated by the ruins of ancient Roman buildings, marking the last time the area had been fashionable. It was here that Don Pietro Pappagallo found refuge and found his niche.

In return for saying Mass daily for the community, Don Pietro was given an apartment with a terrace that overlooked the Eternal City, a small stipend and a devoted, dauntless housekeeper called Maria Teresa Nallo. She was eight years older than Pappagallo and had been born in Fondi, a marshy town on the Appian Way between Naples and Rome that had supposedly been founded by Hercules. How, when or why she came to the Italian capital is not known, but, with her good cooking and gentle chastisement of his idiosyncrasies, she and Pappagallo were a perfect match. In one photograph, Don Pietro sits, beaming, on his terrace, while behind him, allowing the infectious joviality of the priest to spread a thin smile across her lips, stands Maria Teresa, formidable, faithful, and, for fifteen years, Don Pietro's closest companion and confidante.

Quickly populated with basil plants from Puglia, and diffused with the scent of Maria Teresa's excellent cooking, Don Pietro's little terrace became the centre of the neighbourhood, where the pair spent long hours entertaining Pappagallo's fellow clergy with copious bottles of good red wine, putting the world to rights late into the night with local political leaders, or shedding a tear of sympathy over a cup of coffee with a girl from one of Rome's street corners. While the garrulous Don Pietro would play the host, Maria Teresa would bustle around, keeping a careful eye on who came and went and making sure that everything was kept in order – the perfect foil to Pappagallo's more *laissez-faire* attitude. There were, of course, rumours that the chaplain had done what many Roman Catholic clergy have done before and since and taken a wife in all but name. Whether theirs was a romantic or a platonic love we will never know, but it is impossible not to notice the affection between them in those sepia moments on the terrace in Rome. Like her beloved Don Pietro, Maria Teresa was not born great, but as the cleric's life and activities became riskier and riskier, imperilling them both, she never wavered in her loyalty or her love.

The grainy voice over the wireless in September 1939 that announced, in cut-glass received pronunciation, that Great Britain and her Empire were now at war with Germany, must have seemed as far from the Via Urbana as the shot in Sarajevo had felt from Terlizzi. Although we know that he was an avid follower of the news (mostly to provide gossip for his terrace dinner parties), Don Pietro probably didn't even hear it. Despite being the cradle of European Fascism, Italy did not, in fact, enter the Second World War until the summer of 1940. Mussolini had spent the 1930s grand-standing but, unlike his more ideological political allies in Germany, didn't see the war as being a great or worthy struggle: 'I only need a few thousand dead,' he said to his chief of staff, 'so I can sit at the peace conference as a man who has fought.' Little did Il Duce know that victory was far from assured and that, less than five years later, his bloodied corpse would be strung from a lamp post in Milan.

A combination of Mussolini's studied reticence to engage on any front other than ones with clear territorial significance to Italy, as well as the Italian military's consistently incompetent performance, meant that the realities of war did not trouble the Italian peninsula until sometime into the conflict. The Italian government deliberately ignored or mislaid requests from their mighty northern ally to move against their Jewish population, not least because Mussolini's own intellectual mentor, biographer (and lover), Margherita Sarfatti, was herself Jewish. They made only cursory, disastrous moves against British troops in North Africa, and focused considerably less effort on tactical movements than on loud propaganda (including the claim that their bombing of Scotland had been so heavy that the Loch Ness Monster had been killed). On the Via Urbana, Maria Teresa's coffee still flowed on the terrace, the sisters continued their teaching and Don Pietro Pappagallo still said Mass.

✝

All this changed in July 1943. In a series of lightning strikes against what they had correctly deduced to be the weak underbelly of the Axis alliance, British and American troops landed on Sicily and their respective air forces began to bomb Rome. A couple of weeks later, in the face of major Allied gains, the Italian King sacked Mussolini and had him arrested. As he was being transported to prison in September, however, Il Duce was rescued by Nazi paratroopers and installed as puppet dictator over the 'Italian Social Republic' – the parts of Italy not yet under Allied control, an area that included Rome.

The Germans were now in a position to take direct control. They poured thousands of troops into Italy and lost no time in importing their infamous secret police, the Gestapo as well, in order to ensure that all laws against Jews, partisans and others perceived as a threat to the Fascist order could be executed with the utmost speed. Rome became a city under lockdown, as the Germans sought finally to weed out the undesirables left hitherto untouched by Italian incompetence and lack of zeal.

In these final months of 1943, as the Roman winter began to bite, those who had once come to Don Pietro for his jollity, his good coffee or his spiritual guidance began to come to him desperate for help. Don Pietro cannot have thought that he might possibly outfox the Third Reich, but it was not in his nature to say no to anyone in need. And so, confronted with a partisan wanted for sabotage against the Germans, the priest turned forger and put together a false identification card, using what he had in his desk (fortunately for Don Pietro, the Roman Catholic Church loved nothing more than flooding his office with pieces of official-looking paperwork). Against all expectations, the ruse worked – though, in fairness, the infrastructure inherited from Mussolini meant that the Germans were barely capable of keeping on top of essential paperwork, let alone ensuring the authenticity of every pre-issued identity card. Regardless, what began as a trickle became a flood. Jews, anti-Fascist intellectuals, deserting soldiers desperate to get home, Don Pietro helped them all. His little apartment became a veritable factory as he sat in his study constructing new identities for all and sundry, while Maria Teresa bustled around playing hostess, ensuring the often cold and malnourished deserters and escapees were treated to the full force of Roman hospitality. Although Don Pietro was heard to proudly declare that 'all it takes is a stamp and a photograph', sometimes the process would be protracted, as more and more high-profile fugitives sought the clergyman's help. Rather than turn them away, Don Pietro and Maria Teresa took them in, giving them a bed for one night, two nights, a week. In a move that illustrated his almost childlike naïvety, Don Pietro kept careful lists of those that he had helped, almost certainly so he could regularly pray for them. In the end, these names ran into the hundreds. This hive of activity was all the more remarkable given their location – a ten-minute walk from the headquarters of the Gestapo on the Via Tasso, where lists of the very same names were being scoured daily to ascertain the whereabouts of those earmarked for arrest and execution.

Pappagallo viewed his ministry as being for all and his illicit activity simply as an extension of that ministry. This remarkable generosity of spirit was to prove his undoing.

In early January 1944, a young, shy, blond man turned up at the priest's quarters on the Via Urbana. He claimed to be an officer who had deserted Mussolini's puppet army and offered his help to the priest in his endeavours. This was nothing unusual. Don Pietro had built up an impressive network of informers, receivers and spies, enabling him not only to produce identity cards for those wanted by the Nazis, but to assist in smuggling them to safety as well. Maria Teresa immediately took against the young man. There was, she would later say, something clumsy in his manner that she did not trust. Don Pietro calmed her fears with words of priestly wisdom and the young man, one Gino Crescentini, was accepted into Pappagallo's circle. By the start of February, the priest had been arrested and sat, languishing under torture, in the very cells on the Via Tasso from which he had saved so many others. When the Gestapo and their Italian collaborators burst into the priest's apartment to take him away, he was there with several others. In the confusion, Maria Teresa made sure that key documents were removed, hidden in her dress and later burned, in a last-ditch attempt to save Don Pietro from his fate. She could not, however, reach the priest's infamous rubber stamps in time; these objects, that had saved so many lives, also acted as the fatal proof.

Don Pietro was imprisoned on the Via Tasso for months. Every week, Maria Teresa came with a mercy package, bringing clean clothes, medicine and food to the imprisoned cleric, all items that Don Pietro made sure were distributed first and foremost to the other prisoners in his block before taking what remained for himself. On her visits, Maria Teresa watched and waited, observing the comings and goings from the notorious building. On 27th March 1944, she obtained the evidence she needed, making a note of Gino Crescentini strolling out of the building with two plain-clothes police officers. Her testimony was crucial when, less than a year later, Crescentini was arrested and imprisoned by the new democratic government for his part in the betrayal of Don Pietro. In the judgement passed on Crescentini in February 1945, he was referred to as the betrayer of 'the great martyr of the Ardeatine'. Three days prior to Maria Teresa's visit to the Via Tasso, on 24th March 1944, Don Pietro had been bundled into a lorry and transported, with three hundred and thirty-four other prisoners, to the Ardeatine Caves, a network of natural tunnels and caverns just south of Rome. There, in reprisal for a bomb attack on a Nazi unit the day before, they were massacred by the SS.

The killing was messy and haphazard as the SS unit in question was made up of young officers, barely out of training. Their commanding officer had arranged for the unit to drink a case of brandy beforehand to steady their nerves, if not their aim. Amid the smoke and screams and chaos in the caves, as the drunken young officers dealt in death, one figure stood out. Don Pietro Pappagallo calmly blessed the dying, called out comfort to the terrified and prayed for the dead until he too was dispatched with two bullets to the back of the head, delivered as he knelt in prayer.

One of the reasons we know all this was because the man to whom Don Pietro was shackled was Joseph Raider, an Austrian deserter from the Wehrmacht who had been apprehended in Rome under suspicion of being a British spy. As the unlikely pair were caught in a bottleneck caused by the hasty SS attempts to herd too many prisoners into the caves at once, Don Pietro managed to loosen his bonds, and Raider's too. Raider took the opportunity to dive behind a bush at the entrance to the cave network during the chaos and escaped. In an act of selflessness that mirrored so many other similar acts in his life, Don Pietro chose to go into the caves to his death, in order to comfort those who had not been so lucky.

†

The history of Italy during the Second World War is a complex one, the history of the Roman Catholic Church more complex still, yet what stands out about the tale of Don Pietro Pappagallo is his simplicity. His simplicity of devotion to his calling, the simplicity of his pleasures and the simplicity of what he did, stamping bits of paper that ultimately saved lives. Perhaps he learned it from the sisters.

His story served as a redemptive tale for a Church and nation scarred by the horrors of war, with his quiet, brave resistance earning him recognition as a martyr by his Church and as a posthumous hero by his nation. Don Pietro never saw this recognition, nor, sadly, did Maria Teresa, who died in early 1945, not even a year after Don Pietro, some say of a broken heart.

What inspired Don Pietro Pappagallo to do what he did? What led him to make those cards and save those lives? What made him take those risks? How could he take those bullets with such calm? Could it be saintliness? If the history of the saints truly is, as Mussolini thought, the history of insane people, there can be little doubting that the actions of the forger-priest of the Via Urbana were mad enough – brave enough – to qualify.

RESISTANCE IN THE OCCUPIED NATIONS

'I am prepared to suffer still more'

CZECHOSLOVAKIA

— BISHOP GORAZD OF PRAGUE —

'A nation of Gorazds'

In October 1938, Adolf Hitler invaded the Czechoslovakian territory of the Sudetenland. While the liver-shaped strip of land between Prague and Dresden had been awarded to the newly formed nation of Czechoslovakia at the end of the Great War, the vast majority of the population spoke, and considered themselves to be, German. Ethnonationalist tensions had been a feature of life there since the mid-nineteenth century as the bizarre combination of imagined folkloric identity, scientific racism and old-fashioned hatred of 'the other' began to trickle down from the intellectual elite to the general public. By the mid-1930s, the trickle had become a flood, and, enthused by the idea of being integrated into a greater Reich, many of the Sudeten Germans welcomed Hitler's invasion, not caring that it was carried out in direct contradiction of the treaties that had bound Germany since 1919 and of international law. While it may not be a surprise that the politically sympathetic population of the Sudetenland allowed a flagrant act of aggression by a militarising Fascist power, it was more of a shock that the nations which were supposed to enforce international conventions against such a thing occurring – namely Britain and France – allowed it as well.

The Munich Agreement, where Hitler had persuaded the Anglo-French alliance not to intervene by claiming that there would be no further territorial demands made on neighbouring countries by Nazi Germany, had been signed on 30th September and gave the Nazis free rein to occupy Czech territory. Famously, on his return, British Prime Minister Neville Chamberlain waved his piece of paper in the air as he stood on the tarmac at the Heston Aerodrome (now an industrial estate marooned by the M4 motorway) and declared, 'I believe it is peace for our time', a belief that was to be shattered in a matter of months. Less well known is Chamberlain's radio broadcast prior to departing for Munich. In it he referred to Czechoslovakia as 'a far-off country … of whom we know nothing'. Perhaps, given that such sentiments were so freely expressed before the conference, the Czechs do not call Chamberlain's meeting with Hitler 'the Munich Agreement' but, rather, *'Mnichovská zrada'* – 'the Munich Betrayal'.

So it was that the Czechs became the first nation to know what it was to live under the Nazi yoke, often acting as the place where Nazi policies were 'tested' prior to being unleashed elsewhere. The residents of Bohemia and Moravia had long prided themselves on their history of resistance to centralised control – from nurturing Jan Hus to sheltering a fugitive Giacomo Casanova; the sense of a bohemian being someone uninterested in convention didn't spring out of thin air. Theirs might have been a country about which Neville Chamberlain 'knew nothing', but the Czechs were to become well known in Berlin for the dogged refusal of vast swathes of their population to roll over to Nazi diktat. A wander around Prague (or most other Czech cities and towns) reveals the cost of this resistance – round most corners you will be sure to find a plaque affixed to a wall or road sign that reads 'Here fell X in the battle for the country'.

Bishop Gorazd did not wake up one morning in late spring 1942 intending to be one of those heroes. People rarely wake up expecting to perform acts of heroism, least of all bookish clergymen trying to keep a crumbling cathedral in Prague going. The centre of Gorazd's operations was no mastodonic monument to ecclesiastical power but a modest Baroque church dedicated to Sts Cyril and Methodius, tucked down a side street just off Prague's New Town Square. It was from the church, since its purchase and conversion from its previous role as a derelict army storehouse in 1933, that Gorazd had run the Orthodox Church in the newly created nation of Czechoslovakia with very little drama. After all, the place was mainly Catholic: unlike other nations claiming Slavic descent, the Czechs and Slovaks had taken the Western side in the Great Schism, and Catholicism became deeply entrenched when Bohemia, Moravia, Silesia and Slovakia came within the orbit of the regime in Vienna, with its close ties to Rome.

With the fall of the Habsburg Empire in 1918, independence had been proclaimed in Prague and a number of religious figures publicly stated it was time to throw off not only Austrian political structures, but religious ones as well. Many elected to form the Czechoslovak Hussite Church (named after Jan Hus, the fifteenth-century would-be reformer executed at the Council of Constance in 1415), but a small number decided to look east to Bulgaria, Serbia, Russia – and Orthodoxy. Among these new converts was a Roman Catholic priest from Moravia called Father Matthias.

He had been born as Matthias Pavlik in Hrubá Vrbka ('the place of the hardy little willow') in 1879. Hrubá Vrbka is a tiny village nestled within the White Carpathians, a mountainous region between Moravia and Slovakia mostly famed throughout its history for its high concentration of bandits. Somehow, he escaped his somewhat inauspicious upbringing and ended up studying at the noted Catholic University in Olomouc, where, in the early 1900s, having excelled academically, he was ordained as a Roman Catholic priest. But at the end of the First World War, the nation began to reject Roman Catholicism as an Austrian import and look for a more 'authentically Slavic' religion, and Pavlik sought to jump ecclesiastical ship.

Pavlik's potential as a leader for the nascent Orthodox community in the new republic was spotted swiftly. In 1921, he was first made Archimandrite of the Hopovo Monastery in Serbia (a sort of senior abbot), and then bishop in the same year. Pavlik took the name Gorazd when he became bishop of the tiny church; it was the name of the successor of St Methodius, the first missionary sent to the region from Constantinople, thus marking him out as the true successor to the first Christians in the region. It was a bold statement for a man whose church numbered, at most, a couple of thousand people spread across several large provinces.

The primary task that the new bishop had was to create a corpus of theology and liturgy in the Czech language, a job to which he was well suited. He produced vast volumes in order to facilitate Orthodox worship in Czech and Slovak and even managed to find time to produce other academic works, notably writing on the life and death of Jan Hus, the man who had first stirred the spirit of Czech religious and national independence some half a millennium earlier. In Gorazd's work on Hus, he took a cautious view of the man who had, after all, been executed as a heretic, but he did produce a liturgy to mark the day of what the Czech state saw as his martyrdom, as well as writing these reflective lines: 'We think that it is better to live and toil for a great cause than to die for it. But there is nothing greater than to lay down one's life for the Gospel of Christ.' This might have remained a throwaway statement in an obscure academic work forgotten by the centuries were it not for that morning in June 1942 when Gorazd woke up a hero.

†

In 1943, British satirist Noël Coward released a song ironically imploring the Allies not to treat the Germans *too* badly when their defeat inexorably came. Though they hadn't been the best of neighbours in the world, to the other nations of continental Europe, Coward, with tongue firmly in cheek amid the unfolding horrors of war, was sure that a spirit of 'forgive and forget' would prevail once peace came. The BBC felt the humour of the song didn't translate well for those listening in, so barred it from the radio. The Nazis, however, understood it perfectly, placing Coward on a list of people to be eliminated on the presumed invasion of Britain. When the full list was published after the war, the author Rebecca West sent Coward an outraged letter, saying, 'My dear! Just think of the people we would have been seen dead with!'

As Coward well knew, to describe the forces of Nazi Germany as being 'a *little* naughty' to the occupied nations, and in particular the Czechs, was a statement of Swiftian grotesqueness. After Munich gave Hitler the Sudetenland in late 1938, the rest of the country was invaded in March 1939 and became 'the Protectorate of Bohemia and Moravia'. Colleges and universities were closed. Political leaders and members of the intelligentsia were arrested en masse and either executed or sent to concentration camps in Germany itself. The plan for the 'Germanification' of these lands began early in 1940. It was to be achieved through both cultural indoctrination and through the deportation and mass murder of those deemed racially impure or impossible to Germanise – some 50 per cent of the population.

In September 1941, Hitler was becoming frustrated with the man he had installed as 'Protector' of Bohemia and Moravia. Konstantin von Neurath had been appointed to the role in an attempt to pacify international objection to Hitler's annexation in 1939. He was a career diplomat whom the Führer had fired from his role as head of the Foreign Service in 1938 for expressing doubts about his plans for war. He had attempted to reingratiate himself by instituting anti-Jewish laws and agreeing to the execution of protesting students, but Hitler wanted more. Von Neurath was removed and replaced by the infamous 'man with no heart', Reinhard Heydrich, of nose-measuring fame.

Heydrich immediately set to work making sure that the Czechs knew that his fearsome reputation was entirely justified. He was inaugurated at 11 a.m. on 27th September in Prague Castle. By four o'clock that afternoon, Alois Eliáš, the tolerated political leader of the Czech government, had been arrested. By the early hours of 28th September, martial law had been declared across the entire country; by that afternoon, the two leaders of Czech military resistance, Generals Bilý and Vojta, had been summarily executed. By 29th September, he had closed every synagogue in the country and banned non-Jews from consorting with Jews. On 30th September, he declared that, for those arrested under martial law, two sentences were available: summary execution or imprisonment at the concentration camp at

Mauthausen. Of the Czechs sent to Mauthausen, only 4 per cent survived. By the start of October, work had begun to construct the Theresienstadt concentration camp and by 24th November the first deportees had arrived there. Heydrich wanted the Czechs, the Führer and the world to know that he would not be showing any mercy to the nation that he referred to as 'garbage'.

Heydrich was convinced that his iron fist and stone heart would crush all potential resistance. He had declared that 'one day the entire region will be German'. Such was the assumed efficacy of his brutal methods that he would routinely ride in an open-topped car, enjoying the bracing breeze as he commuted between his neoclassical manor house just outside Prague and the hulking walls of Prague Castle, behind which he signed away the lives of thousands. He took it for granted that no one would dare to harm him, but he was wrong. A month after his inauguration, the wheels had already been set in motion for his assassination.

In the little church on the other side of the river from Prague Castle, the world of decrees and plots must have seemed very far away. The day-to-day saying of prayers and pastoral care of the little congregation was taken care of by two clergy, Father Václav Čikl and Father Vladimír Petřek, both bright protégés of Bishop Gorazd. They were ably assisted by lay leaders, in particular the sacrist Václav Ornest and the chairman of the synod, Jan Sonnevend, a senior figure in a number of Prague medical organisations.

After the imposition of Nazi rule, Gorazd had been required to put himself under the ecclesiastical jurisdiction of Archbishop Seraphim of Berlin (also a convert), who, in return for his obedience to the new order, sent him some perfume and incense as a gift. Other than this minor organisational hitch, the Church and Bishop Gorazd might well have continued in wilful ignorance of what was going on around them. However, as with Bishop Gorazd, many of the Church's members had joined Orthodoxy out of an intense sense of national pride and felt that the crimes being perpetrated against the country and people they loved could not go on without response. One such man was Jan Sonnevend, who, through his links with the Red Cross, had become a commander in the OSVO, a Czech resistance group that had its somewhat unlikely origin in a pre-war organisation of sports clubs.

Jan Sonnevend was not the only Czech to believe that something had to be done. Many miles away, in the picturesque English village of Addington, just south of Buckingham, František Moravec, the Czech government-in-exile's chief of military intelligence, was putting the finishing touches to an outlandish and risky plan to remind the Third Reich that, far from being inferior, the Czech and Slovak peoples were not to be messed with. He had handpicked nine Czechoslovakian commandos, who, on the evening of 28th December 1942, were parachuted into the occupied territories with the express order to bring about the death of Reinhard Heydrich. Two of the commandos were dropped over the small town of Nehvizdy, to the east of Prague: a baby-faced Czech bricklayer turned soldier called Jan Kubiš and a stocky Slovak former blacksmith named Jozef Gabčík. Over the next few months, they and the other seven men moved between locations, forming plans for their assassination attempt and making contact with existing resistance operatives, including the OSVO.

In mid-April 1942, Jan Sonnevend was approached by Petr Fafek, a colleague at Sonnevend's 'League against Tuberculosis' as well as a fellow OSVO resistance member, who asked whether Sonnevend might be able to hide some potential fugitives in the near future. Having been frustrated by the efforts of the Roman Catholic Church in occupied nations such as the Netherlands and Poland on more than one occasion, the Nazis, directed by the ever-calculating Heydrich, had most churches belonging to the country's majority religion under close surveillance. The small group of Orthodox believers in their recently restored little church were much less likely to attract notice. Sonnevend agreed in principle and waited until the call came to inform him that the church might be needed.

On 27th May 1942, Reinhard Heydrich is riding in his open-top car as usual, en route to Prague Castle. As they approach the narrow bend near the Bulovka Hospital, Heydrich's driver has to negotiate the apparent collision course of various trams (an occupational hazard of driving in Prague, even today). As he does so, another car pulls up alongside them, and the *Reichsprotektor* comes face-to-face with the assassins Gabčík and Kubiš. Gabčík pulls out a submachine gun, points it directly into Heydrich's face and pulls the trigger – but the gun jams. Heydrich, rather than making good his escape, stands up in his car and pulls out his own gun to shoot back. Meanwhile, Kubiš emerges and succeeds in detonating an anti-tank grenade in the car, ripping apart the metal, fabric and the occupants. Incredibly, neither Heydrich nor his driver is dead. As Kubiš escapes on a bicycle, the wounded Heydrich bellows at his driver to chase Gabčík. Sprinting after him, the driver catches up with Gabčík at a nearby butcher's shop, where the commando manages to shoot the bodyguard in the legs and disappear. Meanwhile, it becomes clear that 'the man with no heart' is very human after all and quite severely wounded. He is taken to the Bulovka Hospital, but, in keeping with the deluded logic that had caused him to order the measuring of the nose of the composer Felix Mendelssohn, it is said that he refuses immediate medical attention from non-Aryan doctors, preferring to wait for physicians of German descent to be found. So it is, due to the purity of his Fascist beliefs (but more prosaically, due to the sepsis that had set into his flesh when Kubiš had succeeded in blasting bits of metal and leather upholstery into it), on 4th June 1942, that Reinhard Heydrich dies.

Although the Butcher of Prague took some time to die, the manhunt for those who had attacked him began immediately. When the news that he had been attacked reached Berlin, Hitler was incandescent and ordered ten thousand of the most senior Czech citizens to be summarily executed. It was only when Himmler pointed out that this would involve a serious blow to the industrial capability of the Reich, at the very moment when the war on the Eastern Front was straining its resources, that he relented. That was not to say that the deed would go unpunished, but the rather awkward fact that there were no suspects to hand was an embarrassment to the Nazi high command. Little did they know that, after hiding in a series of safe houses around Prague in the days immediately following the assassination, by the beginning of June, seven of the original nine agents sent over as part of Operation Anthropoid were concealed in the crypt underneath the Orthodox cathedral of Cyril and Methodius down the side street near the New Town Square.

Not only was the presence of the commandos there initially unknown to the Nazis, it was also unknown to Bishop Gorazd. In fairness to Sonnevend, he had tried desperately to find other monasteries or churches in which he could hide the men, but, in the end, faced with no other viable alternative, he had to resort to his own congregation. Fathers Čikl and Petřek readily agreed, despite the enormous risk, as did Ornest. But the question remained: how to tell their bishop? On 11th June, the clergy and laity finally plucked up the courage to tell Gorazd. While initially shocked, Gorazd made the decision that morning that, not only should the Church continue to hide the parachutists, but that he himself would, as shepherd of the flock, take responsibility for them, aware of the huge risk he now ran and the inevitability of death if he was caught.

Although this unlikely cell of resistance fighters was not exactly accomplished in the ways of people smuggling and espionage, even they realised that the first rule of hiding is to keep moving. Therefore, aware that they were being watched by a specially placed spy in the building opposite (who, it would later transpire, had absolutely no awareness of the goings-on behind the church's Baroque façade), they decided that they would try and move the seven most wanted men in Europe to another monastery on 18th June.

This clerical version of *The Great Escape* never came to pass. On the early hours of the very day set for the moving of the parachutists, the little church was surrounded by nearly eight hundred SS men, with express orders that the seven men should be captured alive. Of the original nine commandos, one had committed suicide when his cover had been blown in April 1942; the other, Karel Čurda, had stayed away from the church, preferring to hide in a safe house and, lured by the promise of one million gold marks to anyone who assisted the Gestapo in finding the assassins, had betrayed his fellow parachutists. Unbeknownst to the men in the crypt, to Sonnevend, or to Bishop Gorazd, the operation had already begun on 17th June as former safe houses were raided and entire families arrested.

An almost day-long gun battle ensued as the Gestapo tried to weed out the seven men. Though hopelessly outnumbered, the commandos put up a valiant fight, with the Germans having to resort to flooding the crypt in order to flush them out. When they did, they found only one man still alive (none other than Heydrich's assassin, Kubiš, who was badly wounded). The rest had either been killed in the gun battle or used their last bullets to commit suicide, denying the Nazis the privilege of taking them alive. If Hitler was to have his show trial, he would need to find defendants elsewhere.

Bishop Gorazd was not exactly a man of the world, but even he realised that reprisals were inevitable. So, in a brave, staggeringly unconvincing attempt to join that long line of those who felt compelled to deceive in the service of God, he sat down at his desk and penned three letters to senior Nazi officials claiming that he, and he alone, had been responsible for the smuggling of the commandos and everything that happened after it, even down to negotiating with British intelligence. We don't know what the acting Gestapo chief in Prague thought when a message bearing the letterhead of the Orthodox Bishop of Moravia and Archimandrite of Hopovo Monastery arrived on his desk confessing to the most elaborate act of espionage against the Nazi regime since the start of the war. But we do know that the Germans were not convinced.

Gorazd had tried to sacrifice himself in the hope that the death of a bishop might spare his church and thousands of his countrymen. In this, he failed. Bishop Gorazd, Father Václav Čikl, Father Vladimír Petřek and Jan Sonnevend were taken from their modest little church and subjected to one of the grandest show trials of the Nazi period at the Gestapo headquarters in the gargantuan Petschek Palace in Prague on 3rd September 1942. The result was never in doubt, and the next day, Gorazd, Sonnevend and Čikl were executed by firing squad at an old firing range just outside Prague. Meanwhile, Václav Ornest was sent to Mauthausen with his family, where they perished. Father Petřek, who, the Gestapo discovered, had also quietly been helping to issue baptism certificates to help Jews escape the Holocaust, as well as hiding other partisans, was shot the next day. The Nazi police chief Karl Hermann Frank said after his execution, 'If the Czech nation is to survive, it cannot be a nation of Petřeks!' He might as well have said 'a nation of Gorazds'. Either way, he would have been wrong.

The most famous of the reprisals for the murder of Reinhard Heydrich was the destruction of Lidice, a small village to the north-west of Prague. On 10th June 1942, long before the Nazis knew where the parachutists were (a day, indeed, before Bishop Gorazd himself knew where they were), a group of German soldiers surrounded the village. They were under orders to eradicate the village. The villagers were split up into groups of men, women and children. The women and children were transferred immediately to the town of Kladno, where they were separated. Most of the women were immediately sent to Ravensbrück concentration camp, with the exception of four expectant mothers who, having had their children forcibly aborted, were sent elsewhere. A small group of the children were selected for 'potential Germanisation' and moved to German families. The rest were sent to Chełmno death camp where they were gassed. The men were taken to a farm outside the village where, having been lined up against a wall, they were shot in groups of five. The Nazis offered clemency to one man, Josef Štemburk, the priest and de facto leader of the village. One of the seventeen children (out of a hundred and five) who survived and eventually returned to Lidice remembered the old man coming to read stories in the school, where, as he turned the pages, the children would pin his flowing cassock to the floor, causing him to trip as he got up, to the amusement of his young charges. The Nazis offered him the chance to survive in return for calming his flock. The cleric refused, saying: 'I will die with my sheep.' He did, and the village was bulldozed.

Gorazd and Štemburk were divided by theology, but they ended their lives in acts of bravery which denied Fascism the absolute control, the absolute victory it sought. They lived out the belief that 'there is nothing greater than to lay down one's life for the Gospel of Christ'. That Gospel was one that meant they didn't run, even in the face of imminent destruction, but, like every good shepherd, felt that it was they who had to lay down their lives for their sheep.

There is a proverb that says that, while other Slavic nations are hardy like oak and need axes to break their spirit, the Czech people are like a willow branch; when pressure is applied, they will bend, and bend, and bend until suddenly they snap back with force. The man born at the place of the hardy little willow might not have snapped back himself, nor were his attempts at hoodwinking those applying the pressure successful, but in his unlikely heroism he more than lived up to the pride of his nation.

The twentieth century was not kind to the peoples of Bohemia, Moravia and Slovakia. After the Second World War came the horrors of Communism, where the cycle of fear, hatred and state-endorsed violence was meted out again on the Czechoslovakian people. They were a nation who knew about sacrifice and, crucially, about survival. Despite the words of Karl Hermann Frank, and, indeed, of Neville Chamberlain, the Czech nation did survive and became famed for its continued indomitable spirit, and, contrary to that prediction made on the shooting range in 1942, it survived precisely because it was a nation of Petřeks, a nation of Štemburks, a nation of Gorazds.

POLAND

— ST MAXIMILIAN KOLBE —

Heroism & Ham Radio

'There's an app for that' is, arguably, the most effective advertising campaign of the twenty-first century thus far – although doubtless there is an adman who is now but a twinkle in the milkman's eye who will come up with a line that will make driverless planes, or powdered dietary supplements, or sex robots the must-have accessory of the 2090s. Back in the earlier 2000s, hot off the back of Apple's astonishingly successful slogan, a number of Churches began campaigns designed to get people praying, entitled, 'There's a Saint for that'. It was a very modern advertising campaign for a very ancient idea. Of course, they weren't wrong; just as every conceivable act in the downward spiral of late capitalism has its own equivalent programme or application, so the manifold objects, acts and abstract concepts that make up human experience have the saint who is supposed to take a special interest in them. Hangovers? There's a saint for that: St Bibiana. Volcanic eruptions? There's a saint for that: St Agatha. Spheksophobia (the fear of wasps)? There's a saint for that: St Friard. Esperanto? Drug addicts? Amateur radio? There's a saint for all of them.

Indeed, in the case of those final examples, there is in fact the same saint for all three. How does an individual end up becoming the patron saint of ham radio, those struggling with narcotics and a made-up conglomerated language? What sort of time on earth could secure patronage of these things in Heaven? The answer lies in the astonishing life – and death – of St Maximilian Kolbe, a Polish Franciscan whose devotion to the Virgin Mary (another saint with a bewildering number of patronages and Heavenly responsibilities) led him from the airwaves to Auschwitz.

As if that eclectic selection of patronages wasn't enough, at the saint's canonisation in 1982, the Pope, a fellow Pole, declared that Maximilian Kolbe was 'the patron saint of our troubled century'. In many ways, the time on earth that earned him such an accolade – from his very typical birth to his extraordinarily untypical death – was bound up with the tragic twists and turns of fate in the first half of that remarkable one hundred years. The world of advertising would have us believe that the icon of the twentieth century is a young Elvis or Marilyn Monroe, or perhaps the Coca-Cola brand or the Empire State Building; either way, when you think of something that defines the twentieth century, a bearded, emaciated monk from central Poland is unlikely to be the first thing that springs to mind. The twentieth century was one of technological advancement but also near-primeval bloodshed. How, then, can an organisation which seeks to propagate a message of eternal hope possibly mark a century of such conflict and contrasts? Well, there's a saint for that: St Maximilian Kolbe.

†

When men in Pabianice, a weaving town in the very centre of Poland, realised, in common with so many expectant fathers, that there was very little that they could do personally to help their offspring into the world, they would run along the muddied and crowded streets in search of the midwife, one Maria Dąbrowska Kolbe. As they rushed towards the little wooden cabin she shared with her weaver husband Julius, the housewives who sat on the porches and verges along the road would cry out to the panicking father-to-be a piece of salutary advice about the midwife's whereabouts: 'If she isn't at home, she'll be in church.'

Twenty four miles from Pabianice lies the Zduńska Wola where, on 8th January 1894, Rajmund Kolbe, son of Julius and Maria, was born – one of the three sons the couple were to have who survived infancy. Like so many who would be affected by the attempts of Nazism to 'cleanse' whole regions and restore an invented concept of ethnic purity to Europe, Maximilian Kolbe had entered a world that was an ethnic, political and religious melting pot. Not long after, they moved to the neighbouring city of Pabianice, around thirty kilometres away. There, as when they had been in Zduńska Wola, Rajmund's German father and Polish mother lived in a town under Russian control where they were devout Roman Catholics among a mixed Jewish, Protestant and Orthodox population. If anywhere represented the Europe that ethnic nationalism sought to eradicate, it was here.

Given the passionate belief of his beloved mother, it was no surprise that young Rajmund was more often found in church than anywhere else, showing a particular devotion to the 'Black Madonna of Częstochowa' – a representation of the Virgin Mary found in the Polish city of that name. This early onset piety did not, however, stop the future friar from engaging in all the mischief that one might expect of a conventional childhood. One day, as his mother scolded the then twelve-year-old Rajmund and his brothers for yet another incident bringing localised chaos to the streets and gardens of Pabianice, she asked, in (perhaps justified) exasperation, what would ever become of her boys. The young Rajmund felt condemned by such a question and so, like the good churchgoing child he was, he went along to his parish church. There, wracked with pre-adolescent guilt, he asked the same question to the figure of the Virgin Mary. To his shock, he received an answer, in the form of a vision which he would recount for years to come, crucial as it was to his later vocation.

As the young Rajmund knelt in remorseful prayer, a vision of the Virgin Mary appeared and offered the boy two crowns, one red and one white. The white one, the apparition explained, symbolised a life of dedicated purity, while the red one was the crown of martyrdom. The Virgin of the vision then gave the young Rajmund a choice: which crown would he accept? Kolbe was to become renowned for his rejection of convention and, even at a young age (with the rules set by the Mother of God herself), he found a way to bend them. He accepted both.

As far as the single-minded young Rajmund was concerned, his destiny was set; now it was simply a matter of how to get there. Just a year later, in 1907, a seemingly providential visit by two Franciscan brothers conducting a mission in Pabianice provided him with exactly the path he needed. The Franciscan order was, in many ways, the perfect fit for Rajmund. Firstly, the austere Franciscan way of life, with its renouncing of property and worldly goods, made his vow to live a life of austere purity a possibility. Secondly, the tendency of the Franciscans to involve themselves on the side of the poor and oppressed, as well as their considerable missionary presence in areas with, at best, a lukewarm attitude to Christianity, increased the likelihood of his being able to fulfil his second vow: that he would be martyred as well. Finally, the order was, of course, founded by St Francis – a figure so stubborn that he even managed to get the Catholic Church to change its mind. Francis's father was a fabulously rich merchant, who, when he discovered that his son wanted to renounce all contact with the world and live a life of simple piety, was more than a little miffed. In an attempt to shame Francis in front of the Church authorities and scupper his plans, he accused him of stealing. In the middle of the trial, the saint renounced his parent and gave his father back all that he had given him – including the clothes he was wearing, thus ending the trial completely naked. Any order founded by such a figure was bound to be a good fit for the headstrong young Kolbe.

So it was that Rajmund (and his brother, who had also been affected by the friars' mission and was, conveniently, named Francis) decided to join the Franciscan order. To do so, the boys had to cross the heavily guarded border between Russia and Austria–Hungary in order to get to the order's regional headquarters in Lwów. The geopolitical demarcations of empires meant little to the two pious teenagers from Pabianice and so, blithely unconcerned about the potential danger, they made their way to the monastery in Lwów and, after some years continuing their education, were allowed to enter the monastery as novices in 1910. On 4th September that year, Rajmund took a new name, Maximilian. When he made his final, life profession as a monk three years later, he added another name, with a casual disregard for gendered nomenclature: Mary.

Whether the monks recognised in the young weaver's son a nascent intelligence or whether they were simply looking for a way to keep the somewhat frenetic novice occupied, Kolbe was sent, in 1912, to further his studies at the Pontifical university in Rome. He studied a whole range of subjects but his favourite was astrophysics; he threw himself into the emerging science with great enthusiasm. In fact, Kolbe, who was showing a determination to see things through to their conclusion, wasn't prepared to stop with the exercises and sums set by his tutors but went one step further and gave a great deal of time to a project of his own, namely designing a spaceship. He even went so far as to try and have his design patented, but the patent office was, regrettably, not interested. Kolbe would have to make do with pushing boundaries on earth rather than the bounds of space for the time being.

Despite his disappointment as a rocket scientist, Kolbe found numerous other projects to fill his time in Rome. In particular, he developed a fixation with the Freemasons. Roman Catholicism and Freemasonry have not always had the happiest of relationships. A Papal ban on Catholics becoming Freemasons had been issued in 1738 by Pope Clement XII, after the Inquisition had a bust-up with some English Masons resident in Florence. After that pontiff was taken from this world at the tender age of eighty-seven (by complications following on from an attack of gout), his successors on the throne of St Peter reinforced his ban, accusing Masons of plotting against the Church and having creeds incompatible with Christianity. One of the predecessors of Clement who reinforced the ban was Pope Benedict XV, the less gouty but equally forceful pontiff at the time of the First World War. In response to his stance, a large group of Masons organised a protest in Rome, while the young monk from Pabianice was resident there. Kolbe later described seeing crowds of Freemasons surge towards the walls of the Vatican with banners depicting the devil triumphing over St Michael and shouting abuse at the Pope.

It was only after a rather unfortunate occurrence in the middle of a football match that Maximilian Kolbe had the time to think over what he had seen outside the walls of the Vatican. Ever the flurry of activity, one of the ways that Kolbe found to divert his surplus energy in accordance with his vow to lead a pure life was to play football with his fellow monks at the 'Vinea', a rest house owned by the friars some twenty minutes from his college. There, one day in 1917, Brother Maximilian suddenly sensed that blood was haemorrhaging from his mouth. He was rushed to see the doctor, who, after prescribing him the cure-all remedy of sleep and figs, informed him that he was suffering with tuberculosis.

Bed rest and the brush with the eternal sent Brother Maximilian's active mind into overdrive. After he was cleared to get up and about again, he hurried to his fellow monks and told them that he would be forming a new organisation, designed to work for the conversion of those opposed to the work of the Church, in particular, the Freemasons. It was to be called the Militia Immaculatae. The somewhat militaristic title was no coincidence – as a young monk, the overzealous Kolbe had believed that the best chance of achieving his double crown was to take up actual weapons, until an older brother managed to talk him out of it. Instead, he became a zealous advocate of the language of spiritual warfare, the waging of war by good against evil. The military parallels in Kolbe's new missionary order were perhaps not surprising given that the world was in the midst of the war to end all wars, a conflict which claimed nearly twenty million lives, one of which was Julius Kolbe, Brother Maximilian's father, who had been hanged by the Russians in 1914.

In 1918, Kolbe was finally ordained a priest. Almost as important was the news that, on 26th March 1919, Pope Benedict XV had formally blessed the work of his new 'militia'. Four months later, Kolbe returned home to a newly independent Polish state. Initially, he was sent to teach candidates for ordained ministry at a seminary in Kraków. However, regular recurrences of his tuberculosis meant that he spent more time in bed than in the classroom. Consequently, in 1922, he turned his attentions full-time to the running of the Militia Immaculatae, in particular running a series of publications printed in its name, moving to the historic city of Grodno in the east of the country and setting up a printing press for that very purpose. Poland was, and in many ways still is, a country with a deep-rooted Catholic identity and religious publications were big business. Kolbe's publication – the suitably militaristic *Knight of the Immaculata* – was no tinpot parish magazine but a publication with a circulation of nearly 750,000. Ironically, one of the publication's primary purposes was to stem the tide of what Kolbe saw as religious apathy.

By the mid-1920s, Kolbe was looking for a new centre of operations. He had a vision for a monastic community dedicated not only to the production of printed material (as monasteries had been for centuries) but to every form of communication possible, all given over to spreading the Christian message and, in particular, fostering a devotion to the Blessed Virgin Mary. As befitted a lover of physics, for Kolbe this had to include the latest radio broadcasting technology and for that he needed purpose-built facilities. In 1927, he found a very old-fashioned solution to his very modern problem when he persuaded a godly aristocrat (one Prince Jan Drucki-Lubecki) to donate a large swathe of land, about forty kilometres from Warsaw, to the Church.

It was here that Kolbe began to build the place he called Niepokalanów, the 'City of the Immaculate'. The name was not just another example of Kolbe's somewhat overambitious vision – the complex he ended up building had accommodation for nearly eight hundred monks, a farm, a repair shop, a volunteer fire station, several printing presses and, of course, a radio station, in which Kolbe took great personal interest. After only ten years, the presses were producing over a million copies of tracts and newspapers monthly, the monks had a commercial radio licence from the Polish government and the twenty-eight-hectare site claimed to be the largest monastery in the world.

Such was the velocity of the project's growth that, after only three years, Kolbe went to the other side of the world to start a similar project there. His attempts in China were somewhat hampered by the country's brutal and bloody civil war, but, undeterred, in 1931, he crossed the sea to Japan and set up another 'City of the Immaculate' in the port city of Nagasaki. He insisted on a site round the side of a mountain, making construction inordinately difficult; the process was made more so when Kolbe, ever transfixed by all things Mary-related, decided that another, almost inaccessible, site on the mountain should be turned into a replica of the grotto at Lourdes. Irritating though this locational pickiness might have been at the time, just fourteen years later, from beyond the grave, Kolbe proved to be the unlikely saviour of his own monastery: the mountainside shielded it from the impact of the nuclear bomb that destroyed the rest of the city.

After another abortive attempt to found a similar community in India, Kolbe returned to Poland in 1936 and threw himself into radio broadcasting, earning his own ham radio call number – SP3RN. Yet, for all Kolbe's confidence in the message of hope, Poland in the late 1930s was not a happy place. It sat, looking nervously to both east and west, worried that one or other belligerent neighbour might squeeze the life out of the adolescent republic. It was only a matter of time before it came to pass.

✝

They could not have been a more starkly different pair: the urbane sham aristocrat, the cut of his hair, the line of his jaw and his sharp suit suggesting (incorrectly) the epitome of Prussian efficiency as he shook hands with the mousy, mustachioed, little one-time commissar, who was wearing a deliberately proletarian jacket. And yet, in that handshake on 23rd August 1939, the unlikely pair – Joachim von Ribbentrop and Vyacheslav Molotov – sealed the fate of Poland and of Maximilian Kolbe. Just a week later, the Nazis invaded Poland. By 5th September, word came to the brothers at Niepokalanów to shut down their operations and flee to the countryside, not least because their deliberately provocative name had already stirred the wrath of the German propagandists. The printing presses stopped and most complied. As Kolbe, now sporting a long greying beard, waved each of them off from the steps of the monastery, he offered them all just four words: 'Do not forget love.'

On 19th September 1939, less than three weeks after the declaration of war, German trucks arrived to arrest the final members of the Militia Immaculatae, categorised as political and religious extremists (though, realistically, for all Kolbe's talk, the closest they came to either was the odd blustering editorial in one of their magazines). This first imprisonment lasted just a couple of months. After it became clear that these were, in fact, monks rather than some sort of warrior order, the Nazis allowed Kolbe and a small group to return to Niepokalanów in December 1939. There they were given permission to continue some printing of strictly apolitical, religious work in return for giving over some of their buildings to the army for storage and committing themselves to helping with the war effort. In the case of the monks, they were expected to provide food; in classic Fascist style, even this activity was monitored right down to its specifics, with each brother being tasked to peel exactly sixty potatoes a day to help produce soup for the troops.

Despite the fact that the imprisonment had made worse his already fragile health, Kolbe managed to find ways of subverting the strict conditions on which his freedom was predicated. As far as he was concerned, there was no line between faith and politics – 'do not forget love' applied as much on the town square as it did in the church. Consequently, he continued to print newspapers – admittedly fewer of them, but with the same zeal as before – as well as covertly producing and distributing anti-Nazi propaganda. He devised a machine to make the peeling of the potatoes a matter of minutes rather than days, and he also began to hide refugees, both Catholic and Jewish, fleeing as the Nazis pushed east. They brought with them tales of massacres and mass displacement as it became clear that the aim of the German war machine was not just territorial expansion but the extermination and subjugation of whole peoples.

This became even clearer as the Nazi military regime now installed in Warsaw began to pass rules against Poles and Jews. Poland, being the ethnic and religious hotchpotch that it was, also had a number of Polish citizens of ethnic German descent who, with typical Nazi forethought, the Reich wished to now include in a greater Germany and so exempt from the persecution meted out to their countrymen. One of these

Polish-Germans was Maximilian Kolbe, who, through his father Julius, was considered to be ethnically 'pure' enough to apply for exemption. The identity that Kolbe valued most in the world was, undoubtedly, his Christian faith, but a clear second was his Polish citizenship. As a child, he and his brothers had been bullied for their German-sounding names, an experience that had affected young Rajmund in particular. Now that the young Rajmund had become Father Maximilian, he was adamant that no one was going to reclassify him as anything other than a Pole. Also, as far as he was concerned, it was his identity as a soldier for the Blessed Virgin that mattered first and foremost, not the opinion of some Nazi genealogist. He was not, as we have seen, a man who was wont to change his mind.

With Kolbe's refusal of the ethnic German privileges, Nazi suspicions were aroused. They tried various methods to catch the recalcitrant cleric out, from impromptu military inspections to check he was complying with the governmental terms to getting a local prostitute to sneak into Kolbe's rooms and seduce him. Instead, the unfortunate call girl got a prolonged sermon about the virtues of celibacy. Kolbe wasn't going to give up his white crown that easily. How anyone could seek to deny their Aryan superiority was beyond the Nazis and so, it was assumed, the stubborn friar sitting in his vast monastic complex must be up to no good.

By early 1941, Kolbe was responsible for a network of several thousand people, including nearly two thousand Jews, hidden in and around the 'City of the Immaculate'. But the net was closing in; not only had a number of the publications printed illicitly in Niepokalanów been traced to the Polish resistance movement, but orders had come from Hitler himself to crack down on any sign of Polish dissent, especially among clergy and intellectuals. From mid-1940, in his Bavarian residence, the Berghof, Hitler had been planning one of the most significant offensives of the Second World War: Operation Barbarossa – an invasion of the Soviet Union designed to solve 'the Russian problem' once and for all. One of the key preparations was to ensure that there could be no possible resistance behind the lines in Poland once the Wehrmacht started pushing east. Consequently, anyone considered slightly suspect was rounded up and arrested. The police came to Niepokalanów for the second and final time on 17th February 1941, arresting five monks, including Kolbe, and shutting the monastery.

At first, the group were taken to the infamous Pawiak prison in Warsaw, where Kolbe underwent brutal torture, including lacerations, beatings and whippings, at the hands of the SS. Kolbe kept to his faith, ministering to the forty or so others kept in the same filthy communal cell. During one bout of torture, the interrogating sergeant snatched the rosary beads from Kolbe's belt and pointed to the cross, asking if the monk 'really believed this rubbish'. Kolbe looked the infuriated SS man in the eye and calmly replied that he did, earning him a severe beating. In classic Kolbe style, he used his time in Pawiak constructively, trying to arrange channels of communication to smuggle in clothes, blankets and food, not for himself but for his fellow prisoners. It became abundantly clear that torture and threats would not break the friar's cast-iron will and so, on 28th May, Kolbe was put on a train heading due south-west, to Auschwitz.

†

There was an ominous silence as the late July sun beat down upon the rows of shaven heads outside barrack 14. It was mid-afternoon and Assistant Commandant Karl Fritsch and SS Adjutant Gerhard Palitzsch paced along the serried ranks of emaciated prisoners, who had been standing there since daybreak, with no task assigned to them aside from watching their meagre rations of thin soup poured down the drain in front of their very eyes. Fritsch and Palitzsch were there for one reason – to select ten men to be put to death. Some days earlier, a group, including a man named Klos, supposedly a baker from Warsaw, who had been in barrack 14, had succeeded in that riskiest and rarest of endeavours – escape from Auschwitz.

It was decided that as they were unable to punish Klos personally to punish his barrack instead. There were sixty men in the barrack, mostly Polish, but from all walks of life. Their number included Franciszek Gajowniczek, an army sergeant who had been taken prisoner of war back in 1939. It also included Maximilian Kolbe, who, remembering his own words to his fleeing monastic brethren nearly two years earlier, had not forgotten love, and had spent the few months he had been in the camp sharing out his food and ministering in the face of unimaginable suffering.

Now it was time for the sixty men of barrack 14 to pay the price for the actions of their erstwhile cellmate. Fritsch and Palitzsch were to select ten men to die, and to die in the most drawn-out and excruciating way possible – they were to be taken to the bunker under nearby barrack house 11 and starved to death. The SS men selected those to die at random and, as they reached the number required, Fritsch pointed the fateful finger at Franciszek Gajowniczek and indicated that he was to join the condemned. Gajowniczek cried out in terror and begged for mercy, imploring that his life be spared for the sake of his wife and children. Fritsch was ready to reward this pitiful display with a beating when out of the line stepped prisoner number 16670: Father

Maximilian Kolbe. Silence descended at the sight of a man stepping from his appointed place, and Nazi and prisoner alike stood, gobsmacked, as Kolbe offered to take the place of Franciszek Gajowniczek.

Not for the first time, the Nazis were dumbfounded by the actions of the gaunt Franciscan. Fritsch went over to Kolbe, keeping his hand on his revolver, convinced that this must be some sort of trap. Fritsch stared him in the face and asked him if he was mad. Kolbe calmly but firmly repeated his request and explained that his life was of less use than that of a man with a wife and children, prompting a by now intrigued Fritsch to ask what his profession was. I am a priest, came the reply. Silence again. After a tense pause, the commandant consented and, in the mind's eye of Maximilian Kolbe, the red crown that had been promised back in Pabianice finally hoved into view.

Kolbe was taken to the cells with the other nine men. After two weeks, on 14th August, the guards went to collect the ten corpses. Instead, they found nine; and one weak, emaciated friar from Niepokalanów, praying. The commandant ordered him to be injected with carbolic acid.

On 15th August, Roman Catholics celebrate the Feast of the Assumption of Mary, when, tradition holds, the body and soul of the Mother of God were received into Heaven. The ash that floated up towards the sky out of the chimneys of Auschwitz on the Feast of the Assumption in 1941 included the last earthly remains of Maximilian Kolbe, the man who, even in that most evil of places, did not forget love.

†

On 10th October 1982, the crowds thronged St Peter's Square in Rome to watch a Polish Pope canonise a new

Polish saint. Among the thousands of Poles who made the symbolic journey (which, as their nation suffered under yet another totalitarian regime at the time, was not an easy one) was a stooped, balding old man in his best suit. It was Franciszek Gajowniczek, the survivor of Auschwitz, come to hear what he had known ever since late July 1941 made official: that Maximilian Kolbe was a saint.

In his homily, Pope John Paul II said that Kolbe had shone 'as a sign of love' in a century of sin and death. The pontiff, less preoccupied by gout or Freemasons than some of his predecessors, put his finger on the purpose of a saint in the Christian tradition: to shine as a light in darkness, to not forget love. The twentieth century was, it is true, the century of the radio, the television, of increased prosperity and of medical advance, but it will forever also be the century of the barrack room, the carbolic acid injection and the crematorium greying the Polish sky with the remains of our humanity. There is, even for all of that, a saint: Maximilian Kolbe.

Hungary

— SISTER SÁRA SALKAHÁZI —

The Feisty Nicotine Nun

Poverty, chastity and obedience. It would be difficult to come up with three values more at odds with the prevailing mores of the twentieth-century West than these. The period that saw the dominance of capital, the sexual revolution and the triumph of the individual arguably viewed all three qualities, extolled as virtues by previous ages, as, at best, bizarre affectations and, at worst, held them in naked contempt. Given this, it is not especially surprising that the twentieth century saw a catastrophic decline in those choosing to enter the religious life as a monk or a nun in Europe and North America. While monks and nuns were once staple, ordinary even, figures in Roman Catholic, Orthodox and even some Anglican societies, they became oddities. Consequently, inappropriate or unlikely nuns have become a staple in the cultural lexicon. From *The Sound of Music* to *Sister Act*, the idea of an individual temperamentally more attuned to the world of nightclubs than the nunnery can be found across films and fiction.

Yet unlikely nuns are not just figures of the fervid and lusty male imagination – there are numerous genuine examples of such individuals. A chain-smoking, one-time atheist tomboy would not, for instance, be the figure that one would necessarily immediately associate with a wimple, but that's exactly what Sára Salkaházi was. She was also beatified by the Roman Catholic Church, putting her on the path to being officially declared a saint. Often, the trope of the unsuitable nun in fiction requires them to prove their worth to their adopted communities – in this regard, Sára Salkaházi conformed wholly to stereotype. Hers, however, was not a redemption achieved by teaching Gospel harmonies to geriatrics or marrying an Austrian submariner. Rather, it was through a series of acts of subterfuge, salvation and, finally, an act of sacrifice that would earn her not only the respect of her religious order, but also the official recognition of both the Church and the Jewish World Holocaust Memorial Centre at Yad Vashem.

Sister Sára Salkaházi was born Sarolta Klotild Schalkház on 11th May 1899 at the very heart of the great cosmopolitan crucible of the Austro–Hungarian Empire, a city known variously as Kassa, Kaschau, Cassovia and (as it is today) Košice. The city was confusingly one of the largest settlements of the part of Slovakia that was in Hungary. Even more confusingly, the town had, alongside its Slovak and Hungarian populations, sizeable Yiddish-speaking Jewish and German-speaking populations. It was into this latter group that young Sarolta was born. Her parents ran the Grand Hotel Schalkház, a palatial neoclassical building that catered for the many travellers who passed through this crossroads of Empire. Like the Habsburg Empire itself, the building did not survive the tremulous twentieth century, but the site is still a redoubtable post of internationalism in what is now an altogether more provincial Slovakian town, occupied as it is by a DoubleTree Hilton hotel.

The young Sarolta, therefore, was born into an environment where she was surrounded by and exposed to any number of fascinating characters and opinions. The little girl who emerged from the gilded incubator of the Grand Hotel was, in the words of her own brother, 'a strong-willed tomboy with a mind of her own'. That is not to say that young Sarolta's force of character came out of nowhere – when her father died, her mother, in a move that attracted some comment, took over the board of directors at the hotel, running it herself in order to keep her children in the manner to which they had become accustomed. The daughter inherited much of her mother's no-nonsense attitude, routinely joining in the rough and tumble of the boys at school, often finding herself on the winning team when a tug of war broke out in the playground. Embracing the role of the tomboy did not, however, mean she suppressed her sensitive side, writing plays and poems in stacks of notebooks throughout her childhood and teenage years.

Her strong will and comfortable upbringing meant she had both the mind and the resources to undertake training as a teacher. The idea of preparing young minds for the world of the future suited the young Sarolta, who was enthusiastically taking part in the monumental transformations that had swept away the old world of the Habsburgs and the gilded furnishings of the Grand Hotel. The First World War had changed much in Central Europe, but perhaps most significantly it changed the role of women. While training as a teacher, Sarolta took up two pastimes that, only a few years previously, would have been unthinkable for a woman in her early twenties: chain-smoking and radical politics.

Many of the young teacher's students were from desperately poor backgrounds and the stories that she encountered transformed the course of Sarolta's life. After only a year in the classroom, she decided, partly in accordance with her recently acquired proletarian political principles and partly because she, as an ethnic Hungarian, refused to swear the oath of allegiance to the new Czechoslovak state formed by the Treaty of Trianon, to leave teaching altogether and to enrol as a bookbinder's apprentice, deliberately taking the most difficult and mind-numbing work in order to better understand the condition of the working poor. After her months in the bookbinder's were over, she moved to making hats. All the while, she wrote up her experiences in a cloud of cigarette smoke, filing them as articles and news reports, largely written in her native Hungarian. Such was her skill that she became a prominent journalist, attracting attention beyond the town limits of Košice and becoming well known in socialist circles in both Czechoslovakia and Hungary.

Though her primary motivations were political, Sarolta Schalkház found herself increasingly drawn to religion as well. She had been a nominal Catholic since childhood – though in her late teens and early twenties had been anything but devout, with public declarations of agnosticism, even flirting with atheism. However, as she spent more time around working-class communities, she felt that it was often the Church, rather than any other organisation, that made the most tangible difference to ordinary people's lives. As she returned to the faith of her childhood, a sense that she might be called to a commitment beyond the ordinary life of a believer began to niggle away at her. She took on the job of editor of the party newspaper of the Christian Socialist Party in Czechoslovakia (a not inconsiderable achievement for a woman at the time) but still felt unfulfilled. She got engaged but, after months of wrangling, returned her engagement ring. For most of the 1920s she juggled two vocations – that of journalist turned socialite, swathed in clouds of cigarette and political intrigue, and that of one called to religious service. Eventually, the latter won out and Schalkház approached a group of nuns to join their order.

†

'How do you solve a problem like Maria?'

So sing the nuns in *The Sound of Music* when confronted with a manifestly unsuitable younger member of their community. It is fair to assume that the Society of the Sisters of Social Service had a similar sort of debate, although probably not through the medium of song, when the young journalist applied to join their number. The order was a relatively new one, having been founded in 1923 by the indomitable Margit Slachta. Slachta was herself not exactly a conventional nun. She had the distinction of being the first woman ever elected to the Hungarian Parliament, having been a prominent agitator for female suffrage in the years leading up to the First World War. Alongside her dedication to the religious life, she ensured sisters were trained in nursing and midwifery and, like her new would-be novice, she ran her own newspaper, *The Voice of the Spirit*. Yet even for the order with this astonishing, high-achieving figure at its heart, the whirlwind of a woman from Košice who presented herself for entry into their ranks represented a step outside their comfort zone.

Sára Salkaházi (she had Magyarised her name) had first encountered the sisters when investigating their work with marginalised women in urban areas across Greater Hungary. The idea of a religious order with such a clear focus on helping those who had first stirred her social conscience seemed to answer her prayers. The nuns were initially less keen; though they were active in social justice, prayer and contemplation were pretty high up their list of priorities too – and the nicotine-fuelled bundle of enthusiasm that had just turned up on their doorstep didn't seem a natural fit for poverty, chastity and obedience.

Sára Salkaházi was not, however, a woman to allow a little word like 'no' to get in her way. She became more devout and even managed to give up smoking – a process which she later said was the most difficult thing she had ever done in her life. She applied to the nuns again and again until, in 1929, the sisters finally relented and allowed Sára to enter the order as a novice, eventually taking her initial vows as a nun at Pentecost 1930.

Perhaps unsurprisingly, the community managed to find a reason to send her away from the mother house in Budapest relatively quickly. Sára was sent back across the border to Košice, where she was given a job in the Slovakian national Catholic Charities office. Sára was not, however, going to allow herself to be limited to a regional secretary's role. Instead, she taught, cooked in soup kitchens, coordinated Catholic charitable efforts across the nation and found time to establish and edit a periodical aimed exclusively at women, one of the first Catholic publications of its kind. It was a tall order, even for someone with Sister Sára's reserves of energy. The sheer volume of work eventually got to her and, after a few years in Slovakia, she returned to the community in Hungary, having suffered what would now be considered a nervous breakdown.

The breakdown was devastating to Sister Sára in two ways. Firstly, it took her away from her work with the groups of isolated women that she had grown to love and, secondly, it imperilled her very vocation. Many of the sisters had long held the view that Sára was temperamentally unsuited to the religious life, that her boundless energy and endless projects were nothing more than attention-seeking and that, frankly, she would be better off returning to her fiancé, her secular employment and her cigarettes. The breakdown seemed to confirm all that the naysayers had predicted about Sister Sára's vocation and so, when it came for her to renew her vows made at Pentecost 1930 and become a full member of the order, her superiors turned the application down. She was not, in their view, ready.

It was a devastating blow. The sting of the rebuke probably contributed to Sister Sára's decision, in the late 1930s, to seek a role as a missionary in Brazil, where a group of the sisters had gone out some years before to help alleviate the desperate poverty in its burgeoning cities and towns. Fortunately for the Sisters of Social Service, she never went – the Second World War intervened. She continued to live the life of a nun without her vows until, moved by her obvious commitment, the order relented and, a year after rejecting her, admitted her as a nun, finally allowing her to take her lifelong orders at Pentecost 1940, exactly ten years after she had made her first vows. She adopted a motto at her life profession, taken from the Prophecy of Isaiah: 'Here I am! Send me.'

†

In 1941, Sister Sára was put in charge of the Hungarian Catholic Working Women's Movement, an organisation which was a lot more accomplished at social work than it was at devising catchy acronyms. She was now directly in charge of nearly ten thousand members spread across the country in two hundred and thirty local branches, all involved in direct social work among the poor and the outcast. Quite the responsibility for someone who, just a few years earlier, had been turned away from her order because of her unsuitable personality. Indeed, it would have been a sizeable task even in years of peace and comfort; it was even more so as the Second World War began to make its presence felt in Hungary.

Admiral Miklós Horthy's nationalist government in Budapest was playing its dangerous game of bluff with the Axis powers – trying to avoid too much commitment to a war that the tightrope-walking old politician knew couldn't be won and yet wanting to use alliances with Fascist regimes to shore up his own repressive government. (Horthy's primary qualification for leadership had been winning one of the old Austro–Hungarian Empire's only considerable victories of the First World War, crushing the Italian fleet at Otranto while lying wounded on a deckchair.) A key bargaining chip in the Admiral's risky and ultimately unsuccessful strategy was Hungary's Jewish population. Although he stopped short of extraditing Hungarian-born Jews to die in Nazi camps, he did deprive them of employment, meaning that more and more became dependent on the goodwill of their Hungarian neighbours, and, in particular, on charities run by organisations such as the Catholic Working Women's Movement.

In some quarters of Hungarian Christianity, there was (as there was in various Churches across Europe, to their shame) a clear reticence to help those of a different faith as the desperation of the Jews increased. This was not the case for the projects managed by Sister Sára. Following the express instructions given to the whole society by Sister Margit herself, she did all she could to shelter Jewish people through her official work, opening the Working Girls' Residential Homes, which her institute ran, not only to destitute young women but also to large numbers of Jews under the threat of persecution.

Yet, despite her vows of poverty, chastity and obedience, there was enough of the old maverick Sarolta left in the person of Sister Sára to go one step further. Alongside her official efforts as part of her order, Salkaházi was involved in dangerous personal attempts to save the lives of those who had been declared socially undesirable and 'unworthy of life' by the Nazis. The advantage of her job was that it gave her a good excuse to cross the border to the newly independent Slovak Republic (where there was still a sizeable Hungarian minority population, many of whom were part of the movement).

While Horthy's Hungary had prevaricated when demands came to advance Fascist principles relating to race purity, the government of Slovakia had embraced them with open arms. The Slovak People's Party had spent the interwar years trying to secure greater autonomy for the Slovakia region from the Czechoslovak government in Prague. The failure of the international community to react when Hitler invaded the Sudetenland in 1938 emboldened the nationalist movements in Bratislava to make common cause with the Nazis in order to break away from Prague. In 1939, when Hitler turned the western half of Czechoslovakia into the Protectorate of Bohemia and Moravia, the eastern half became an independent country, and a staunch ally of the Nazis. The two leaders of the SPP became prime minister and president; the former was a radical and rabidly anti-Semitic law professor called Vojtech Tuka, the latter was a podgy and charismatic ukulele enthusiast named Jozef Tiso, who, alongside his political career, was a Roman Catholic priest.

Tiso's government was, however, anything but cuddly, and it was certainly not conducted along the lines of loving thy neighbour. The Slovak government enthusiastically

volunteered large swathes of its Jewish population for deportation into the hands of the Nazis as early as February 1942,
with Tiso even giving a speech in the west of the country to
encourage the deportation of Jews. Many of his fellow Slovak
clergy were outraged. The Vatican made a formal complaint.
Even Adolf Hitler commented with some surprise, 'it is
interesting how this little priest is sending us the Jews!' For
Tiso, however, as with a number of Christians across Europe,
anti-Semitism and the Christian faith were disconcertingly
easy bedfellows.

Whatever the priest-president of Slovakia thought, Sister
Sára took a radically different view. Seeing the beginnings of
the deportations in Slovakia over the course of 1942, by 1943
she was involved in an elaborate operation bringing at-risk
people over the border to the comparative safety of Hungary.
Her legitimate reasons for travel and her easy access to nuns'
habits (so very often the perfect disguise) made her the ideal
people smuggler. It is thought that she single-handedly saved
at least a hundred people, mostly young women without any
other help to turn to, while the order as a whole saved well
over a thousand.

However, Hungary could only remain a comparatively
safe environment for so long. Salkaházi knew it would not
be long before what she had seen in Slovakia would spill
over the border. In the Slovak Republic, the processes of the
Holocaust had been aided and abetted by one prominent
clergyman and Sister Sára was adamant that when the
Nazis inevitably lost patience with Horthy, her vows to the
religious life would win out over any pressure that could
be exerted by the barrel of a gun. So, on 14th September
1943, Sára Salkaházi made a solemn vow to God, at her
own request, in the presence of the Mother Superior in
Budapest. She pledged that she would offer herself up as a

sacrifice to save both the other members of the order and those that they had concealed in convents and safe houses across the country, should their shelter ever be threatened. She believed, absolutely, that the risky work of hiding and helping the despised was nothing short of the work of God and, in typical Sára Salkaházi style, she was adamant that nothing should get in its way.

†

The hour of judgement for Horthy, Hungary, and for Sára Salkaházi, was not long in coming. On 15th March 1944, German troops entered Hungary in order to 'safeguard her sovereignty'. That day, Sára Salkaházi was celebrating, although not because of the military and political changes that were in motion. In order to keep her spirits up during hours of clandestine travelling across borders and between safe houses, Sister Sára had written a play about the life of St Elizabeth of Hungary, a woman who had used a position of power and influence to serve the poor and needy despite secular pressures. Needless to say, there were more than a few barely concealed allusions to the situation in Europe present in the script. Perhaps, in particular, Sister Sára had the corpulent clergyman sitting behind the president's desk in Bratislava in mind.

The play's premiere was to be its final performance as well. The Nazi invasion saw a crackdown on newspapers, theatres and other forms of cultural expression, as well as an instant increase in the number of Jews, disabled people, gypsies, homosexuals, political and religious dissidents and other undesirables deported on trains bound northwards for the killing plains of occupied Poland. As the persecution intensified, so did the efforts of the Sisters of Social Service to shelter those earmarked for extermination; and as these efforts increased, so too did the chances of the authorities noticing, and, therefore, of Sister Sára's pledge becoming a reality.

In October 1944, even the avowed anti-Communist Horthy, who had been a puppet leader since March, realised that resistance against the Russian forces now pressing at Hungary's borders was futile. As he negotiated a surrender, he was removed in a German-backed coup (being forced to sign his resignation at machine-gun point) and replaced as Hungarian leader by the senior figure of the Arrow Cross movement, an ultra-nationalist Fascist group. The new leader was one Ferenc Szálasi, a soldier turned politician, who, in a strange coincidence, had been born just a stone's throw from the Grand Hotel Schalkház in Kassa in 1897, two years before Sister Sára.

Szálasi's period in power was short and bloody. He ensured that all those who had been spared by Horthy's incompetence and prevarication were efficiently handed over to the control of the infamous Adolf Eichmann. However, by December 1944, the Red Army was already pressing towards Budapest. Szálasi had practically no control, even over the capital, where mobs of Arrow Cross vigilantes began a programme of horrific violence. As law and order broke down completely, Szálasi, like any good Fascist, preoccupied himself with minutiae – making an exhaustive list of streets and buildings in Budapest named after Jews and proceeding to give them new, Hungarian names one by one.

Meanwhile, the Arrow Cross indulged in an orgy of violence across Budapest, as the tanks rolled ever closer, aiming to 'liquidate' the city's Jewish population before the inevitable surrender to the Soviets. They started by entering the city's hospitals and poorhouses, butchering people in their beds. They then turned to those institutions that were suspected of harbouring Jews, with convents and monasteries high on their list. Christmas 1944 was a bloody one in Budapest, as death squads of Arrow Cross militiamen stormed hostels, churches and monastic houses, determined to kill any 'undesirable' they could find, and willing to kill anyone else who got in their way.

In Western Christianity, 27th December is celebrated as the Feast of St John the Evangelist, the 'beloved disciple' of Jesus who, though he prayed to be martyred, ended up living out his days in contemplation and asceticism as 'a martyr of will, but not of deed'. Sermons preached on his feast invariably dwell on what it is to be a martyr. In the context of Budapest's bloody Christmas, and with her own pledge of the previous year in her mind, it is not surprising that, when Sister Sára was asked to lead a reflection for her fellow nuns on the morning of 27th December 1944, she chose martyrdom as her subject.

A key part of Sister Sára's daily routine in those fractious and violent months was to tour the various safe houses under her jurisdiction in Budapest, in order to check that all was well and to replenish supplies. She was returning from just such a visit with another sister when they saw that the mother house was being raided by the Arrow Cross, on the hunt for fresh victims after a tip-off by a disgruntled domestic worker. Rather than return to another safe house, Sister Sára marched up to the men who were inspecting the papers of the residents, demanded that they answer to her as director and was arrested.

A number of women had taken refuge in the house's small chapel, where, above the altar, a single golden candle indicated the presence of the Blessed Sacrament. One later described how, as they sat cowering, the doors were flung open and, framed by the lintel, the unmistakable figure of Sister Sára appeared, flanked by two somewhat bemused Arrow Cross militiamen. 'Let me in here,' she said, with such an authority that the two vigilantes momentarily relaxed their control, allowing her to surge towards the tabernacle in which the consecrated host was kept. There she knelt for a brief moment, with the light of the candle reflecting on a face that was wrinkled, not by years of care but by regular laughter. The moment lasted only a second or so, but in it, the eyewitness said, there was a tangible sense of peace. Sister Sára was prepared now to keep her vow. The Arrow Cross men broke the moment seconds later, roughly pulling the short, dark-haired nun up from her prayer, telling her there would be time to pray that evening.

That evening, however, rather than being given time to pray, Sister Sára, one of her lay colleagues and four of the Jewish women that she had hidden, were taken to the banks of the River Danube. Alongside her sisters, Sára Salkaházi knelt down, made the biggest, broadest sign of the cross she could and was shot.

Today that embankment is named after Sister Sára Salkaházi. The order (which, of course, had originally rejected her) recognises her sacrifice as having saved thousands of other lives, and the Roman Catholic Church has beatified her, setting her on the path to sainthood. Not exactly the fate one might have expected for a chain-smoking, atheist tomboy. Probably not the fate she expected either. By contrast, Jozef Tiso, the 'pious and excellent' student who became the successful politician and president, is remembered as a collaborator. The all too successful priest versus the unlikely, unsuccessful nun.

Tiso and Salkaházi between them represent the compromised, confused and complex relations between Fascism and the Roman Catholic Church. Both ended their lives at the hands of executioners: one for helping to kill thousands of innocent people and the other for helping to save thousands of others. They both grew up in the bosom of Habsburg Christendom: one responded to its collapse by embracing the jackboot and rifle butt, the other by embracing prayer and social work. Both flirted with radical politics: one doubled down on that embrace, the other realised her fellow humans were invariably better served by other means. They both took Holy Orders: one lived up to her vocation, the other failed his.

The strains of Johann Strauss II's 'By the Beautiful Blue Danube' are, for many, the evocation of that gilded Habsburg Christendom in which Tiso and Salkaházi were born. The river itself flows through Vienna, Bratislava and Budapest, three capitals that saw many of the monumental changes of the twentieth century that make that Habsburg world seem so far away, including the rise of Fascism and Communism, and the terrors that both those ideologies wrought on the people that live by the banks of the beautiful blue Danube. Today, as each three of those capitals face the rise of unrest again – from murdered journalists to the creeping rise of autocracy – the banks of the Danube might well see some of the same horrors in the twenty-first century. If so, it is to be hoped that the Churches might respond in the spirit of Sister Sára Salkaházi, rather than in the spirit of Father Jozef Tiso.

THE NETHERLANDS

— CARDINAL DE JONG, KOENO GRAVEMEIJER & ST EDITH STEIN —

The Ecumenism of Blood

I n the thin, south-eastern strip of the Netherlands that sits between Belgium and Germany there lies a town called Roermond. It was here, in this unassuming corner of the province of Limberg during the year 1888 that Jonkvrouw van Aefferden had arranged to be buried next to her husband, one Graf Colonel von Korkum, who had gone to meet his Maker eight years earlier. So far, so bourgeois. There was, however, one issue. Graf Colonel von Korkum had been a Protestant and so had been laid to rest in the town's Protestant cemetery, with a plot next to its neat stone wall. On the other side lay Roermond's resting place for its Roman Catholic dead. The stones of that wall represented communities that were totally separate in life, and wished to be so in death (although, of course, under-ground, the worms were free to dart between Catholic and Calvinist corpses, depending on what tantalised their taste buds that day). The division was such that even the wishes of the ailing Jonkvrouw couldn't overcome it. Or so people thought. The widow duly died and was buried, not in her family vault in the centre of the graveyard, but, to the surprise of staid, convention-bound Roermond society, on the other side of the wall, just feet from her husband. The funerary monument that she commissioned was even more surprising. It consisted of two graves of equal height; from the top of each came an outstretched hand, sculpted in stone. These two hands clasp in the middle, just over the top of the neat stone wall, mocking its attempt at division and ensuring that death did not part them.

The tale might seem to have been lifted out of a collection of sentimental late nineteenth-century short stories but it serves as a convenient illustration of two points. Firstly of just how conventional Dutch society was in the period leading up to the mid-twentieth century, and, secondly, of the extent to which confessional identity divided the Dutch people, even in death. Catholics and Protestants were, with the Liberals and the Socialists, part of the 'four pillars' of Dutch society. They had their own political parties, their own schools, their own newspapers, their own pubs – even, as the story of the widow of Roermond shows, their own graveyards. They did not mix in private, they did not mix in public. Intermarriages, like that of the Colonel and the Jonkvrouw, were rare and attracted considerable attention. The system was known as 'pillarisation': a nation where sectarianism manifested itself not in hatred or violence (though prejudices undoubtedly existed) but in minding one's own business without engagement or even proximity to those of a different identity. It would take something even more drastic than the will of Jonkvrouw van Aefferden to shake up the highly segregated Dutch society. It would, in short, take a war, and a war, at that, that was to threaten the very existence of the Dutch nation, with all its divisions and idiosyncrasies, itself.

When Britain and France declared war on Nazi Germany in September 1939, the attitude of the Dutch government was very much 'Here we go again.' In the First World War, the Dutch had declared a speedy neutrality and had then spent the rest of the war desperately hoping that the superpowers busy blowing each other to pieces would continue to do so in Belgium. Their battle plan in 1939 was much the same. But this was a very different war – gone were the Kaiser and the Tsar and their gentlemen's agreements. To Hitler, ideologically bent on reshaping Europe and the world according to the new Fascist order, Dutch neutrality was not worth the paper on which it was written. After the period known as 'the phoney war', German operations began in earnest in the spring of 1940. On 10th May, the sound of Messerschmitt engines above the flat plains of Holland heralded the beginning of Operation *Fall Gelb*, the Nazi plan to swiftly knock Belgium, Luxembourg and the Netherlands out of the war before progressing on to conquer France. The Dutch armed forces put up a valiant attempt at resistance but were overcome – due to cost-cutting, they had not conducted any summer exercises between the years 1932 and 1936 and nearly half their hundred and fifty-strong air fleet were antiquated biplanes, a sizeable proportion of which were non-operational. Queen Wilhelmina, who had been evacuated (somewhat unwillingly) by a British naval ship when, on 13th May, defeat became an inevitability, set up a government-in-exile in Britain. Later, on denouncing her Prime Minister Dirk Jan de Geer for trying to arrange a negotiated peace with the Nazis, Churchill called her 'the only real man in London'.

With Wilhelmina fulminating in a town house on Piccadilly, and the elected politicians divided between her supporters and those looking for negotiated peace, a great gulf of leadership opened in the Dutch nation. Suddenly, with the Wehrmacht on every street corner, the old pillars of Dutch society didn't look so important after all.

✝

The pair of men who were destined to help end pillarisation were not the most likely candidates, not least because one of them, Koeno Gravemeijer, had historically been one of the system's fiercest advocates. Gravemeijer was born in 1883, the son of a Dutch Reformed pastor. It was no surprise to his family when the studious and serious Koeno announced his desire to follow in his father's footsteps. Yet, as we have seen, religious identity was closely intertwined with other aspects of life in the late nineteenth-century Netherlands. The teenage Koeno soon developed a political infatuation with the Calvinist political superstar of the day, Abraham Kuyper. Kuyper, too, had been a pastor but, by the start of the nineteenth century, had risen to become Dutch Prime Minister and was an ardent advocate of the pillarised system. By the time Gravemeijer rose to prominence, his political hero was long dead, but the varying reactions to the Nazi invasion even within the old Prime Minister's own family show just how divided parts of the nation were. His son was a fierce Dutch nationalist and, as a result of the Boer War, harboured a pathological hatred of Britain. He collaborated and joined the SS, only to freeze to death in the abyss of the Eastern Front. Kuyper's granddaughter, by contrast, spent the war organising and hiding Jews from the very death squads her uncle so publicly supported.

It wasn't only Kuyper's family who ended up abandoning his carefully thought-through political categorisation of Dutch society. Despite the official neutrality of the Netherlands, as with so many other figures in this volume, Gravemeijer had been appalled by the barbarism of the First World War. The doe-eyed, bookish hero-worshipper of the 1910s became the zealous, energetic, politician-cum-pastor of the 1920s. Gravemeijer became convinced that what the world needed was not a pillarised society, with its slow drift towards a disinterested intellectual modernism, as well as the technological modernism that had led to the mechanised horrors of the Western Front, but, rather, a society that was explicitly Christian. In 1920, he left the sleepy suburb of Voorburg where he had served as a pastor in a small church and took up a role in a congregation in the very centre of The Hague, putting him at the heart of the Dutch political scene.

By 1921, he had founded his own political party, dedicated to the advancement of Calvinism, a cause which enjoyed remarkable electoral success among the doggedly sectarian voters of the Netherlands (enabling Gravemeijer to become a thorn in the side of successive Liberal and Conservative governments). Not only were his politics and his faith strictly Calvinist, but his entire mode of being was organised along strictly Reformed principles. Gravemeijer was a walking embodiment of the Protestant work ethic. He was involved almost constantly with schemes and projects both religious and political. He had few hobbies and fewer friends. He could be unsympathetic to those who failed to keep up with his punishing work rate – while his ox-like constitution and sheer bloody-mindedness would help him get through four years in a concentration camp, they weren't exactly qualities conducive to getting on with his colleagues. It was a surprise, therefore, when, in April 1940, just a month before the German invasion, Koeno Gravemeijer was elected (by the narrowest of margins) to be Secretary of the

Reformed Synod and so became the pre-eminent Protestant religious figure in the country.

In ordinary times, Gravemeijer would have almost certainly spent his tenure on the constant bickering that is internal Church politics; but ordinary times these were not. The regime that the Nazi invaders implemented represented everything that Gravemeijer loathed: the rhetoric of progress towards a glorious Fascist future grated with his instinctive hatred of modernism; the cult of personality around Hitler enraged his positively Old Testament sensibilities around idolatry; and the regime's desire to impose a Fascist reading on every aspect of life, from school curricula to religio-racial characterisation on medical forms, went against everything he had spent his career fighting for. It was little surprise then when, in the summer of 1940, the headstrong pastor gave orders for all Church organisations, in particular schools, to fire anyone 'tainted with the blemish of National Socialism'.

Displaying his characteristic verve and energy, Gravemeijer followed this up by telephoning around his colleagues and publishing statements for them to read out from their pulpits, condemning Nazism as utterly antithetical to membership of the Church and to the message of the Gospel. Such bull-in-a-china-shop tactics didn't last long and, by the spring of 1941, less than a year into his tenure as leader of the nation's Reformed Churches, Gravemeijer had been locked away where he could protest no more, namely in a concentration camp in the south-eastern part of the country, where he spent the rest of the war frustrated and increasingly embittered. After the war's end he was an isolated and profoundly cynical figure, blaming all the world's ills on 'idealism', including, retrospectively, his own. However, his arrest was not for nothing: he provided a very different man with just the excuse he had been looking for to bulldoze his colleagues and launch an unprecedented public attack on the Nazi regime.

Johannes de Jong was the Archbishop of Utrecht and, by virtue of that role, the senior Roman Catholic in the Netherlands. Both in terms of religious belief and temperament, he and Gravemeijer could scarcely have been more different. Archbishop de Jong had come from humble beginnings as a baker's son to being one of the pre-eminent figures in Dutch national life. He had been born in 1885 on the island of Ameland, a strip of sand in the North Sea that was split between a small Catholic settlement on the east of the island and a small Protestant settlement on the west. The two communities had spent the three hundred or so years since the Reformation quietly fuming at one another in a way that only small-town dwellers can. An upbringing in this environment of quiet mutual loathing perhaps went some way to explain the considered reserve, even *froideur*, which seemed to characterise de Jong's interpersonal relationships. Many thought him ill-suited to the role of leadership – he was a bookish intellectual, who had spent several years writing lengthy and, frankly, tedious treatises on Church history before his rapid elevation to the senior gig in the Dutch Catholic Church in 1936. Yet after his promotion, de Jong began to show signs of a fiery disposition.

When he had come to the Archbishop's throne, there were many in the Netherlands (including Koeno Gravemeijer) who expected the withdrawn ex-professor, with his funny islander accent and bad eyesight, to make no impact whatsoever. Almost his first act as Archbishop was to excommunicate anyone found to be a member of the NSB (the Dutch sister party of the Nazis). In practice, pillarisation meant that most NSB members were part of the less formally organised Liberal pillar, as opposed to the Catholic one. However, de Jong's action had a measured effect, with the vote share for the NSB halving at the elections in 1937.

In the summer of 1941, after the arrest of his unlikely brother-in-arms, de Jong reissued this statement to be read out in every pulpit in the country, along with extra punishments for any found collaborating in even minor ways and a wide-ranging condemnation of the actions of the Nazi regime. The Church, the letter said, 'could no longer be silent'. Breaking this silence was to have huge costs for many Catholics across the Netherlands, not least for de Jong himself, who was now on an inexorable collision course with the occupying regime.

The Ridderzaal is a rather florid Gothic edifice in the middle of The Hague. Originally built as a banqueting hall for the Counts of Holland, it went through a series of uses, until, in a fit of late nineteenth-century medieval revivalism, the Dutch government reappropriated it for use as the throne room where the monarch would officially open Parliament. However, back in May 1940, it was not the doughty Queen Wilhelmina who made her way to the ornate seat of state to address the nation but a uniformed Austrian with a pronounced limp. This was Arthur Seyss-Inquart, newly appointed *Reichskommissar* for the Netherlands, a former lawyer turned paramilitary and politician whose commitment to Nazism, and its anti-Semitism in particular, had caused him to play a crucial role in turning the Austrian government over to Hitler's direct control in 1938. Seyss-Inquart made it his stated aim to bring about the total Nazification of Dutch society, down, as he put it, 'to the smallest chess club'. Given such an aim, it was little surprise that he soon imprisoned the inflexible Gravemeijer, and yet it was de Jong who was to become his avowed enemy.

The relationship between the two men didn't exactly start well. After Seyss-Inquart made his speech in the capital, demanding loyalty from the Dutch people to their new masters, de Jong put out his own statement. Given that the occupying forces aimed to stamp the swastika on everything down to the very school textbooks, the Archbishop stated that no declaration of loyalty would be coming from the cathedral in Utrecht any time soon. De Jong had been frustrated by the failure of many of his own bishops to be forceful in their opposition: the cautious and elderly Bishop of 's-Hertogenbosch, Monsignor Diepen, had already watered down de Jong's statement against anti-Semitism for fear of kindling Seyss-Inquart's wrath. And so, in the summer of 1940, he broke the old Dutch rules of society and contacted Gravemeijer and other senior Protestant figures in order to develop a coordinated Christian opposition to the Fascist regime.

De Jong also found other ways to circumnavigate the timidity of some of his episcopal colleagues. He joined forces with the bombastic Monsignor Lemmens, Bishop of Roermond, who had publicly announced in July 1940 that he would rather be martyred than fail to resist the Nazis, and would shout at German soldiers he saw that 'in the end Christ would conquer' them all. Together, they began to launder money through the 'Fund for Special Needs' to help smuggle resistance fighters to England, to assist downed RAF pilots to return across the North Sea and to help Jews and partisans hide in Dutch homes. However, by the summer of 1941, the arrest of Gravemeijer and others, as well as the first trainloads of Jews departing the Netherlands for Buchenwald and Mauthausen, meant that even cautious bishops could turn a blind eye no longer. The Church agreed to let de Jong complement his covert resistance with a further public condemnation: the letter in which he stated he could no longer be silent.

Silent was exactly how the Nazis would have preferred him, of course. On the night of Saturday 2nd August 1941, the telephone in the Archbishop's residence in Utrecht rang, and rang, and rang. When the Archbishop's bleary-eyed secretary finally picked up the phone, it was Seyss-Inquart, demanding that de Jong immediately cancel the reading of the letter that was planned for the following Sunday morning. De Jong refused, calmly finished his cocoa and went to bed. The next day, a number of clergy were dragged from their pulpits and altars and off to prison. Seyss-Inquart officially announced the annexation of all Catholic social groups to the control of the NSB, and the Archbishop himself was issued with a gargantuan fine for his actions. Seyss-Inquart had wanted him imprisoned or, better still, shot, but even he knew his limits. The actions of the *Reichskommissar* in August 1941 only served to strengthen de Jong's hand – he was now the undisputed leader not only of Catholics in the Netherlands, but of Christian and arguably the wider resistance as well.

By November of that year, de Jong was chairing a covert meeting of Church leaders, both Catholic and Protestant, who were concerned about the escalating anti-Jewish actions of the occupying forces. Seyss-Inquart had a pathological hatred of Jewish people himself and, eager to please Hitler, had begun introducing anti-Semitic measures in early 1941. By April 1942, he had ordered the construction of a ghetto in Amsterdam; a couple of months later, the mass deportations east began. Increasingly aware of the trajectory across Europe, the group of Church leaders approached de Jong to help draft a text pleading Seyss-Inquart for better treatment for Dutch Jews 'in the name of Dutch Christendom'. On 11th July 1942, the combined Catholic and Protestant group (itself an astonishing achievement given the polarisation that prevailed only three years earlier) sent a telegram to the *Reichskommissar* to be forwarded to the German government, condemning in the strongest possible terms the treatment of Jewish people by the occupying forces and their collaborator colleagues. Anti-Semitism was, the text said, 'contrary to the deepest moral sense of the Dutch people' and was 'against the commands of God to justice and mercy'. 'We urge you,' the telegram said, 'not to execute these measures.'

Seyss-Inquart was in a quandary. Never before had such a cross section of community leaders in an occupied territory made such a strong statement against the Third Reich's anti-Jewish measures. The advantage of pillarisation was that the Church leaders could feasibly claim to speak for about three-quarters of the Dutch population – if they were to make their statement public, the line he'd peddled to Hitler about the Dutch being willing participants in a union of Aryan-Germanic races would clearly be shown to be nonsense and he'd be forced to act against the nation's most powerful institutions. Doubtless there was also, lingering at the back of his mind, the memory of his previous humiliating public spat with de Jong – the last thing he wanted was to give the wily Archbishop another propaganda victory. After three days of equivocation, the *Reichskommissar* told the Church leaders that he would waive the deportation order for those ethnically designated as Jews who could prove they had been members of a Christian Church prior to 1st January 1941 – provided the Churches did not make the telegram's incendiary text public.

Some of the leaders were satisfied with this seeming compromise on the part of the *Reichskommissar* and advocated complying with Seyss-Inquart's demand. Johannes de Jong was not one of them. Instead, with understated but steely resolve, he persuaded the Churches to go still further, coordinating a mass public reading of the denunciation on Sunday 26th July and composing a prayer for better treatment of the Jewish people to be recited alongside it. Again, Seyss-Inquart got wind of the plan, again the phone rang at the Archbishop's palace, and, again, de Jong, with an aristocratic hauteur that belied his humble origins, ignored it, not even informing his brother bishops of the *Reichskommissar*'s protest, considering it a foregone conclusion that any attempt to interfere with what was read out in his pulpits would be ignored. Eight of the Protestant denominations who had joined with de Jong in drafting the telegram held firm as well. And so, as the bells called the Dutch people to their many and varied places of prayer on the morning of 26th July, the message across denominations was the same: an explicit, public condemnation of the early stages of the Reich's Final Solution.

Word of the protest spread fast. In the *Reichskommissar*'s office in The Hague, an Austrian limped quickly round his office, ranting and raving in fury at what had occurred. In an office in the Chancellery in Berlin, another Austrian did much the same thing. Some weeks later, in a hotel room just off Piccadilly, a fat, elderly woman clapped her hands with joy at the first signs of her country turning to resist the men who had deprived her of her throne, while a prisoner in a camp near the German border allowed an uncharacteristic smile to escape his pursed, Protestant lips when he realised he had not been alone in his protests. In the residence at Utrecht, the Archbishop said Mass, then spent the rest of the day with his beloved books. In the cemetery in Roermond, the graves of the Jonkvrouw and the Colonel still stood, while, in their respective churches, both the theatrical Roman Catholic bishop and his more restrained Protestant counterpart for the first time ever read the same words in a show of unity against a common foe. A nun, under that same bombastic bishop's personal protection, listened to the letter being read out, clasped her rosary and steeled herself for what was to come.

The nun was Sister Teresa Benedicta of the Cross, a Carmelite nun in the town of Echt, just west of Roermond. She had been born Edith Stein to a German-speaking family in western Poland and, more significantly, she had been born a Jew. Sister Teresa Benedicta had had a glittering career as a secular academic philosopher, having been awarded a doctorate with the highest possible honours at the age of twenty-four. She held a series of teaching positions throughout Poland and Germany, producing a seminal translation of the works of Thomas Aquinas and engaging in debate and study with the pre-eminent philosophers of the time, from Husserl to Heidegger. Yet it was her study of another great female thinker, St Teresa of Ávila, that prompted her conversion to Christianity. In 1933, while a professor at a university in Münster, she wrote a letter to Pope Pius after witnessing the horrors of early Nazi pogroms, warning him that 'responsibility falls on those who keep silence in the face of such happenings'. She received no reply.

She did, however, receive an invitation from a Carmelite convent in Cologne to join their order, the same one as her heroine, Teresa of Ávila. This she did and it was through them that she was able to escape a Nazi arrest warrant, with her sister in tow. In 1942, she was visited by her friend and confidant Bishop Lemmens. Used to regular displays of ecclesiastical exaggeration, she was surprised when he soberly and seriously offered her the chance to go into hiding using the network of partisans and priests that he and de Jong had helped set up. Despite the bishop begging her, she refused, instead beginning to train herself to endure periods of hunger and cold, aware that, as Seyss-Inquart plotted revenge on the Church for its resistance, her name would be near the top of the list.

In a macabre mirroring of the moment of de Jong's triumph, the *Reichskommissar* ordered that, as the bells rang for Mass on the morning of 2nd August, Sister Teresa Benedicta and two hundred and forty-four other Christians of Jewish descent from across the Netherlands (including the nun's sister, Rosa Stein, who had managed to flee with her to Echt) should be seized and taken to concentration camps in Amersfoort and Westerbork. From there, a number, including Sister Teresa Benedicta, boarded trains leaving the country on 7th August. Watching the nun calmly providing care and comfort to her distressed fellow prisoners so moved a Dutch official tasked with helping them onto the trains that he offered her the chance to escape. Once again, Sister Teresa Benedicta was resolved: nothing would stop her from sharing the fate of her brothers and sisters. As her train passed through the town of Schifferstadt in Germany later that morning, she managed to leave a message there for the nuns of the town to pass back to her own order, saying simply, 'We are going east'. At some point on either 9th or 10th August, Sister Teresa Benedicta of the Cross, née Edith Stein, entered the gas chamber at Auschwitz–Birkenau and was killed.

The deportation of hundreds of Christians and thousands of Jews, as a direct result of his protest, haunted de Jong. On one level, Seyss-Inquart had won: he realised that de Jong cared nothing for his own safety (being, like Bishop Lemmens, more than willing to undergo persecution and even death), but by striking at the very people the Archbishop was trying to protect, he had delivered a gut-wrenching wound to the would-be resistance leader. The *Reichskommissar's* political victory did him little good in the long term. As the Allies advanced on the Netherlands at the end of 1944, Hitler ordered him to enact a scorched-earth policy, a matter on which he deliberately equivocated, realising that the German position was now futile. As famine gripped the Netherlands, he reluctantly agreed to allow British and US planes to conduct food drops to help the starving population, while himself refusing to surrender. His stubbornness prompted the American commander, General Walter Bedell 'Beetle' Smith, to inform him that 'whatever happens, you're going to get shot', prompting Seyss-Inquart to reply that such frankness 'left me cold'. 'Yes,' replied the American, 'it will.'

De Jong's nemesis found in Bedell Smith and the Allies a new enemy he couldn't beat and, in 1946, he was executed at Nuremburg. A little over fifty years later, one of the people he ordered to their death was honoured with sainthood in a ceremony at Vatican City and, to mark the horror of the continent's history, was named there as one of the patron saints of Europe. That person was Sister Teresa Benedicta, now known as St Edith Stein.

The decision by the Dutch Church leaders to condemn the Nazis is remembered as a costly failure. And so it was

– for the two men themselves, as well as for innocent men and women like Edith Stein. Gravemeijer's imprisonment affected him deeply. He became disillusioned, ending up in self-imposed exile, isolated and unpopular, giving tacit support to a South Africa that was slowly enacting many of the same rules against 'the other' that had characterised the Fascist regimes of Europe and which, as a younger man, he had so rigorously opposed. Cardinal de Jong found his clergy and his laity deported and executed, then suffered the decline of both his own health and the health of his Church. In the autumn of 1942, he suffered a debilitating stroke, brought on through overwork, then a serious car accident, silencing him in a way that the *Reichskommissar* never could. He was awarded a cardinal's hat for his resistance efforts, but no amount of scarlet could restore his health, and he died in 1955, still mulling over whether he had been right to resist.

And yet it would be a mistake to see the protests of Gravemeijer and de Jong as a disaster, given their united influence. It gave the Dutch people permission to break the societal bonds that had been hardwired into their culture, the sort of bonds that separated the Jonkvrouw and the Colonel all those years before. It gave them permission to engage in some of the most astonishingly brave acts of resistance to the forces of Fascism seen in Europe during those dark days. Catholics and Protestants, who had lived so separately, engaged in such resistance and often died together. A new unity was born: an ecumenism of the blood. Thousands of Dutch people, Christian and otherwise, reached out across those seemingly impenetrable boundaries and helped those in need in small, personal acts of resistance, just as the grouchy, determined Protestant minister and the quiet, bookish cardinal had appealed for them to do.

One such person was a certain Miep Gies, who lived in Amsterdam for the duration of the Nazi occupation. Miep was a Roman Catholic lay woman who had been born in Austria. She came to the Netherlands as a child, fostered by a Dutch Catholic family who showed her that 'kindness was a medicine as much as the bread, marmalade, and the good Dutch milk, butter, and cheese'. It was she who helped hide a family in the attic of a house in Amsterdam, it was she who smuggled them that same bread and cheese to keep their strength up, and it was she who, in 1945, handed the diary she had managed to hide from the Gestapo to Otto Frank, father of Anne, enabling her story to be shared with the world.

GREECE

— MOTHER SUPERIOR ALICE-ELIZABETH, PRINCESS ANDREW OF GREECE AND DENMARK —

A Tale of the Crown & the Wimple

In early May 1941, a shiny Mercedes pulled up outside the elegant Athens town house owned by Prince George of Greece. George was a not unimportant figure: the son of one King of Greece, the brother of a second and the uncle of a third (the unfortunate King Alexander, who died after getting into a fight with a monkey) and a fourth (the only scarcely more fortunate George II, who had been forced into exile on three separate occasions). However, the pair of jackboots that stepped out of the car and onto the doorstep that spring day had not been polished as a show of deference to the house's royal owner but, rather, in honour of one of his guests. George had generously agreed to let Alice, the wife of his feckless and wayward brother Andrew (who was spending the war in Monaco with his French mistress), reside there, after he discovered that she had been living in a two-bedroom apartment in downtown Athens.

When Nazi forces finally captured the Greek capital, on 27th April 1941, it was only a matter of time before they made their way to find Alice, who had been born Princess of Battenberg and whose daughters had married the Prince of Hesse and the Margrave of Baden, both officers in the Wehrmacht. As members of Germany's old aristocracy (most of whom were, at best, frosty towards the new Third German Empire that Hitler was trying to forge), their presence in the Nazi forces was a great propaganda coup. Consequently, when it was discovered that their mother-in-law was living in a newly conquered city, the Nazi high command immediately dispatched a high-ranking officer to pay a social call.

Whether this scion of the Wehrmacht had been briefed before his visit about the Princess's character is not known. Either way, he clearly felt that a combination of old Prussian deference and modern German charm was what was required to win over a woman who, however straitened her wartime circumstances may have been, was still a great-granddaughter of Queen Victoria. As they sat taking coffee in Prince George's rooms, the Nazi leaned in and, with the air of a strapping young nephew deigning to visit an aged relative, asked the little old lady perched on the chair opposite whether there was anything he could do for her. Her little eyes, sunk into a sparrow-like face, narrowed, looked him up and down, from his Brylcreemed hair to those oh-so-carefully polished boots, and replied, in a cut-glass German accent the general could only dream of, 'Yes. You can take your troops out of my country.' And with that, she left the room.

To demand the unilateral withdrawal of Hitler's forces in the presence of a senior Nazi was gutsy, but this astonishing display of aristocratic sangfroid was the least of the little old lady's achievements. From hiding Jews to distributing food, winding up the Gestapo to nursing the injured, the exploits of Alice of Battenberg, the Princess turned would-be nun, as she struggled against Fascism in her adopted home of Athens, were all conducted with a glint of steel behind her beady stare and with a devout faith in her heart.

†

'He hath put down the mighty from their seat, and hath exalted the humble and meek'

This is the manifesto at the heart of the Magnificat, the song that is sung by the Virgin Mary in the Gospel according to St Luke and is at the heart of numerous Christian liturgies, from the chanted antiphonal hymn used in morning worship across Eastern Orthodoxy to the thousands of settings that exist for its use in Anglican Evensong. Yet, for all its centrality in worship, it points to a tension that Christianity has never really managed to resolve: what is its relationship with power?

In AD 312, just before the Battle of the Milvian Bridge, the Roman emperor Constantine had a vision of the cross in the sky and, after winning the battle, converted to Christianity – a faith that had, until that point, been the creed of a tiny and brutally persecuted minority. By the time of the Edict of Thessalonica in AD 380, the faith that had started with the judicial murder of its leader by the Romans had become the state religion of the Roman Empire. A faith that had developed much of its credal identity on the margins of power now found itself at the centre of the most important political entity on earth. To say this presented something of a theological quandary would be an understatement. Ought Christians to reject the trappings of power or embrace them to do good? Many groups maintained (and still do) that Christianity's default political position must be one of absolute radicalism, rejecting power structures of any kind – a line of thought that led, several centuries later, to the somewhat farcical sight of well-meaning Anglican Vicars trotting over to Russia in order to praise the government of Joseph Stalin, whom they naïvely saw as the Virgin Mary's best bet.

This tension exists not only in the abstract world of theology but in the lives of individuals as well. Of course, in some cases – men like Jozef Tiso, or Tomás de Torquemada, the instigator of the Spanish Inquisition – it has led to abuses of power in order to justify what they felt to be the right path. In other cases, the marriage of humility and power has been more creative, from Thomas Becket to Oscar Romero. Perhaps the strangest example of this contrast was found in the figure of a women who was born at Windsor Castle on 25th February 1885 but who died having given all her possessions away; who was christened with the title 'Her Serene Highness' and with the Queen-Empress Victoria as a godmother but who would later take the name Sister Alice-Elizabeth as an Orthodox nun; who had seen her world utterly destroyed by the First World War, and who spent the latter part of her life resisting the new world that Nazism was trying to forge in the Second World War.

The young Alice had an equally astonishing childhood, in the middle of an inordinately complex network of inter-marriages around the extended family of the British Queen. As a child, the young Alice was carted between Germany, Britain and Malta by her parents Prince Louis of Battenberg and Princess Victoria of Hesse and the Rhine (the European monarchy may have had many qualities that made them preferable to dictators, but creativity with names had been bred out many moons ago). Very early on, as the toddler Princess displayed clear difficulties with speaking, it became clear that Alice was, in fact, deaf. Rather than view this as a reason to cast the child aside and focus on her healthy siblings, her mother and grandmother ensured she was given the most advanced medical care as well as special tutoring, including being taught how to lip-read. By the time she was a teenager, Alice could lip-read and speak English, French and German fluently. At the age of seventeen, she added Greek to that list of accomplishments after it was announced she was to be married to Prince Andrew, the seventh child of George I, a middle-ranking Danish prince who had been invited to become King by the Greeks in 1863 when their previous monarch proved to be less than satisfactory.

The marriage was not an especially happy one. Although the couple were united by their shared love for Greece and her people, they were of quite different temperaments. Prince Andrew was a dashing, impetuous cavalry officer, famed for sleeping with almost everyone – male or female – whom he encountered. By contrast, Alice, now known by her husband's name of Princess Andrew, threw herself into charity work and, as her mother had, took an earnest interest in her children, of whom there were to be four girls and one boy, Philip, who, as a young man, would go on to win the heart of Princess Elizabeth, the heir to the British throne. A significant incident in the early years of the couple's marriage was their trip to Russia in 1908 to attend the wedding of a Russian princess and a prince of Sweden. There, Alice saw her aunt – the German-born Grand Duchess Elizabeth Fyodorovna – for the first time in many years.

Elizabeth had been married to Grand Duke Sergei of Russia until he was blown to pieces by a revolutionary terrorist in 1905. After her husband's death, she became intensely religious and threw herself into acts of charity, eventually giving all she had away and becoming a nun, starting her own order of sisters dedicated to providing medical care to the very poorest. Her efforts earned her the particular hatred of Vladimir Lenin, who said of her that 'virtue with a crown on is a greater enemy to the Revolution than a hundred tyrant Tsars'. When the Revolution came, Lenin personally ordered her murder. She and a number of companions were taken outside the town of Alapayevsk and thrown down a mine shaft, followed by a number of grenades. Somehow, Elizabeth survived this ordeal and was heard by the Bolshevik men to be singing hymns from the bottom of the pit. They responded by filling the shaft with bracken and setting it on fire. The Grand Duchess's setting down of the gilded tiara and picking up of the wimple, as well as her later stubborn refusal to flee when her adopted country came under the sway of murderous ideologues, was to make a lasting impression on her niece.

The Russian Revolution wasn't the only political upheaval to shake Europe in the early years of the twentieth century, and Greece had more than its fair share of unrest. In 1909, troops at the Goudi barracks in eastern Athens revolted, leading to a coup espousing similar ideas to the so-called progressive nationalism that had recently swept the ailing Ottoman Empire. As a result of the reforms, led by a group of officers dissatisfied at the traditional way in which the army had been run, Prince Andrew lost his military commission and was forced back to civilian life. This period on Civvy Street was short-lived; in 1912, as the region – Greece included – descended into the warm-up for the First World War – the Balkan Wars – Andrew was reinstated to a command post (though, admittedly, to the somewhat back-seat job of running a field hospital), while Alice threw herself into nursing work. A year later, the country was in turmoil again as Alice's father-in-law, King George I, was assassinated. A year after that, the mechanised slaughter of the First World War commenced, with one side of the Princess's family pitched in total war against the other. By 1917, her brother-in-law, King Constantine, was forced to abdicate in the face of fierce protests against his policy of keeping Greece neutral as Europe ripped herself apart.

Alice and her family fled as well, spending most of their time in Switzerland in what was to be the first of many exiles. In 1920, after the unfortunate monkey-induced death of King Alexander, King Constantine returned to Greece and reappointed his brother Andrew to a military role. Alice spent most of this time on Corfu, where, in 1921, her last child of five, Philip, was born. The return did not last long and, after a failed military expedition against Turkey (in which Prince Andrew's refusal to follow orders during the pivotal Battle of Sakarya attracted particular criticism), Andrew, Alice and their children were forced into exile once more, this time to Paris, where, to their anguish, they were treated as Danish, rather than Greek, citizens.

The family settled down into a relatively humdrum existence in the suburbs of the French capital. Alice became even more devoted to charity work, even spending after-noons doing shifts at a second-hand shop devoted to raising money for refugees from the continuing crises in Greece and Asia Minor. This increase in her philanthropic endeavours was accompanied by a greatly heightened religiosity, inspired by the memory of her now martyred aunt Elizabeth. After contact with the Greek Orthodox Cathedral of St-Étienne in Paris, on 20th October 1928, Alice gave up her Protestant faith and followed her aunt into the Orthodox Church.

Not long after, she began to experience dramatic visions, including one where she was informed by Heaven that she was to develop healing powers. Her husband, and many others, believed she had gone mad. In 1930, as her family was dispersed across Europe – with her daughters marrying into what remained of the German Royal Houses, her son sent to boarding school in England and her husband eloping to the Riviera with his French actress mistress – Princess Alice was committed to the Bellevue clinic at Kreuzlingen in Switzerland where, she was informed, she would be treated for her mental breakdown. Despite the sanatorium's exclusive reputation, her royal status did not mean that she was treated any more kindly than other patients with mental health issues were at the time. The centre's director, a Dr Binswanger, who had authorised her forcible removal from her family, diagnosed her with paranoid schizophrenia. Another doctor who examined her case was the famous Sigmund Freud. He, unsurprisingly given his own obsessions, decided that it was sexual frustration and recommended subjecting the unfortunate Princess to a series of X-rays designed to radiate her ovaries out of existence and so suppress her libido. Predictably, given such treatment, Alice loathed her time in Switzerland and made several attempts to escape. Her protestations of sanity eventually won out and in 1932 she was released.

After a brief stay in the Tyrolean spa town of Merano to recuperate from the horrors of her treatment, the Princess, now estranged from her husband and out of touch with her children, spent five years wandering aimlessly around Europe. Financed by various handouts from relatives, she stayed in bed and breakfast establishments in decaying resorts, living among her own thoughts as the continent around her descended into madness. Despite Dr Freud's extreme treatment, her visions persisted. Once, as she sat on the terrace of a Cologne boarding house where she regularly stayed, gazing into the sky, the son of the couple who ran the establishment came over and asked what it was she was looking at. 'St Barbara' came the reply. She was jolted out of this blissfully low-profile existence in 1937 when, as it had so often before, tragedy stuck her family. Back in 1931, her third daughter, Cecilie, had married the Hereditary Grand Duke of Hesse. It was a happy marriage and, by late 1937, the Grand Duchess was heavily pregnant with her fourth child. The little family (with the exception of the youngest child, Johanna) boarded a plane on 16th November to attend a family wedding in London. As the aircraft approached the Belgian port of Ostend, fog impeded the pilot's sight, sending the plane careering into a factory chimney. Everyone on board was killed.

The news was enough to bring the dispersed family back together again. The funeral was to be the first time she had seen her husband in nearly seven years. It was enough, too, to jolt Alice out of the strange, transitory existence that had seen her float around Europe. Despite being united in grief, no reunion between husband and wife was forthcoming. If the intention of Alice's time in Switzerland was to 'cure' her of her religious beliefs, it had had the opposite effect. If anything, she now clung to her faith more than ever, to the extent that she would never have countenanced divorcing Andrew, despite his flagrant infidelity while she had been at her lowest ebb.

Now that, in the never-ending carousel of Greek politics, the monarchy was back in Athens in the person of her husband's nephew (another George), she decided to move back to one of the few places she had felt an affinity with in her restless existence. A living husband meant that a nunnery was not an option and so she purchased a poky two-bedroom flat in the Kolonaki district of Athens and gave herself over to good deeds. She had planned to take her teenage son with her but was dissuaded when it was pointed out that a continuation of his schooling in Britain would probably do him more good than living in a spartan flat in an Athenian backstreet. Had Alice got her way, the history of Britain would have been notably different. Two years later, when he was still a cadet at the Royal Naval College, he was tasked with chaperoning the young Princesses Elizabeth and Margaret and so was set on the path that would lead him to become, in the words of the honorific bestowed by the Pacific Tanna islanders, 'man belong Mrs Queen'.

Though she returned to Greece without her son, Alice was not left in peaceful isolation for long. In 1939, Fascist Italy conquered Albania as part of Mussolini's deeply unlikely plan to build a new Roman Empire with himself as a second Caesar. As with the Romans, it was only a matter of time before Mussolini stretched a chunky, grasping hand towards Greece and, on 28th October 1940, Italian troops invaded, bringing the Second World War to the Greek lands. As was so often the case during the conflict, the reality of the Italian war effort fell rather short of their dictator's strutting and posturing and the Greek forces, with some British support, managed to turn the tables and themselves invaded Italian Albania. Hitler, fearing that Britain had found the weak underbelly of Fortress Europe, poured German troops into the area and, by April 1941, the Greeks had been beaten back and their capital occupied.

As war began to take its toll on the Greek population, Alice and her sister-in-law Elena Vladimirovna (a cousin of the murdered Tsar) decided to remain when most of the other royals took up the British offer to evacuate them to Cape Town. Both Elena and Alice looked to the example of Grand Duchess Elizabeth during the chaos of the Russian Revolution and decided to join the Red Cross. They moved into their brother-in-law's house together and began nursing the sick and injured, setting up soup kitchens and caring for those orphaned as a result of the fighting. The sight of the two old ladies, offspring of the crowned heads of Europe, marching with great confidence into Athenian neighbourhoods that no policeman would dare enter bemused the occupiers when they arrived in 1941. But, as that smooth Prussian general mentioned earlier, the Gestapo and many others were to discover, they underestimated Alice and Elena at their peril.

Those links to the crowned heads of Europe were to come in handy for Alice, giving her, as they did, an excuse to travel across the war-torn continent with a degree of diplomatic protection and to receive parcels that otherwise would have been treated with suspicion. She marshalled her siblings into helping her in her efforts to alleviate the suffering of Athens' poorest people. When she was allowed to visit her sister, Louise, who was married to Crown Prince Gustav Adolf of Sweden, Alice (never one for overly close relations between family members) spent most of her visit collecting food and other supplies for the Red Cross, returning to Greece with her luggage stuffed full of aid parcels. She also nagged her younger brother Louis for a steady stream of packages, pulling at his heartstrings with tales of her own privation when, in fact, she would distribute them directly among the poor of Athens. This was all the more remarkable when one considers that Louis was not only splitting his time between Britain and America but, as Lord Mountbatten (the anglicised version of the Battenberg name), was playing an instrumental role in the Allied war effort against Germany.

As the baking Greek summer of 1943 finally came to an end, so too did the Italian occupation of the majority of Greece, including the areas directly around Athens (the Germans having considered the capital itself too important to be given over to Rome). As Mussolini's government fell, the Germans moved swiftly to occupy the areas that had been under the jurisdiction of their unfortunate southern allies. By the end of August, just under fifty thousand of the country's seventy-five-thousand-strong Jewish population had been deported from Salonika to Auschwitz. Those who managed to avoid deportation frantically roamed the country trying to find refuge from the death trains that were shunting their friends and family north.

One such group of desperate refugees was the Cohen family. Haimaki Cohen had been a prominent Greek MP, who, just when the popularity of the royals was at a low ebb, showed kindness to King George I by sheltering him during a flash flood. In return, the King had promised that, if ever there was something the Cohens needed, they had only to ask. Haimaki himself died at the start of the war, with the royal offer unclaimed (not that they would have been much use in Switzerland). He left a widow, Rachel, and five children. As the Nazis began to round up Jews in the summer of 1941 so began a desperate race against time to flee to safety. Freddy, the eldest son, managed to arrange a crossing of the Mediterranean Sea for himself and his two elder brothers to join the Free Greek forces fighting with the British in North Africa, but his mother, sister Tilda and brother Michel were stuck in Greece, with the threat of deportation to certain death growing more likely every day.

Freddy had heard stories about the strange, steely, devout Princess who had refused to leave Athens in the city's hour of need. With his options running out, his father's seemingly unlikely boast of the promise of royal favour was as worth a try as anything else. Royal favour, as far as it existed in Greece in 1943, was vested in a pair of difficult little old ladies sitting in a draughty town house surrounded by nurses and icons. To say it was a leap in the dark for the Cohen family would be an understatement. Somehow, Freddy made contact with Alice and, to his surprise, she agreed to hide his mother, sister and brother in the attic of the town house. On 15th October, two huddled, terrified Jewish women were bundled into the back of the Princesses' house; a little later, they were joined by Michel and there they remained, safe, for the duration of the war.

Despite her persistent rudeness to members of the Nazi high command, Alice was treated with a certain dignity, which generally allowed her to flaunt the rules. Direct disobedience of a Nazi race law, though, was a step too far and, although she had succeeded in saving the Cohens undetected, the ever-watchful Gestapo soon smelled a rat at the residence of the Princess of Greece and Denmark. Their suspicions were compounded by the fact that Alice's son, Philip, was now known to be serving with the British navy; once again the jackboots were at Alice's door, except this time the Prussian charm had been well and truly dispensed with. However, if the Gestapo thought they would succeed in their attempts to intimidate the Princess (who, after all, had suffered two years of torture at the Bellevue sanitorium), they were, time and again, sorely mistaken. Expecting the sparrow-like figure to give in immediately, they began questioning her about her links to social and racial undesirables, only to be met by stony silence. After several more questions, Alice decided to put the faltering secret policemen out of his misery and proclaimed, 'I am deaf and can't hear what you're saying.' The normal methods of intimidation and physical violence were, in this case, out of the question and so, in an unusual reversal of roles, the interrogators left with their tails between their legs. Alice, and the Cohens, were not bothered again.

Even when the Nazis were finally pushed out of Athens in October 1944, Alice made use of her deafness to wave aside officialdom. The liberation had come at an enormous cost and her work doling out food and medical help to the sick of Athens was even more critical than it had been before. As the Nazis withdrew, opposing groups of partisans and resistance fighters (as well as British forces) converged on the Greek capital, all hoping to seize the initiative in shaping the nation that might emerge from the chaos after the war. In a desperate attempt to keep order in the fractious city, the British introduced a strictly enforced curfew. Sentries, however, reported that the order was being repeatedly flouted by one particular offender: Princess Alice, who, having ignored Nazi attempts to stop her visiting the poor and needy, saw absolutely no reason why she should pay attention to the British. Eventually, an officer took her aside and warned her that there was a very real risk she might be accidently shot if she carried on with her nocturnal relief missions. Alice, fixing him with exactly the same avian glare with which she had stared down the German general in 1941, replied, 'They tell me that you don't hear the shot that kills you; and in any case I'm deaf, so why would I worry about that?'

Though it didn't get her shot, her parcel distribution did affect her health in another way. Food was scarce over the winter of 1944–5 and almost anything edible that came Alice's way was distributed to those who were, as she saw it, in greater need. Indeed, when the future British Prime Minister Harold Macmillan (who was serving as the de facto British governor of the liberated territories around the Mediterranean) paid a visit to her in the autumn, he wrote a note back to Whitehall expressing concern that the great-granddaughter of the Queen-Empress Victoria should be living in such 'squalid' conditions. For several weeks that winter she ate nothing but bread and, in a letter to her son, confessed that she could scarcely remember the last time she had eaten meat. Despite these privations, her faith remained resolute; she might have ended the war physically frailer and more gaunt but, spiritually and in her own iron determination, Alice was as tough as ever.

Aside from her heroism, the war brought one very significant change to Alice's life – in December 1944, she learned that she had been widowed. It was somewhat ironic that Alice, who had put her life at risk from Gestapo death squads or stray British bullet hundreds of times, managed to survive the war, whereas her husband, who had spent the entire conflict in a suite at the Hotel Metropole, Monte Carlo, failed to see out the conflict courtesy of an enormous heart attack. With her husband gone to meet his Maker,

Alice finally believed herself able to serve hers in the way she had long felt called to do and, after raising the necessary funds to start her own order (even the truculent Alice had enough self-knowledge to realise that putting herself under someone else's jurisdiction would not have ended well), she became a nun in 1949. She took the name Alice-Elizabeth in honour of the aunt who had long inspired her.

Her family, never the most sympathetic to her religious beliefs, were less than impressed. Her mother (by this point at the well-past-caring age of eighty-seven) exclaimed, 'Whoever heard of an Abbess who smokes and plays canasta!' – a reference to Princess Alice's well-known love of both Woodbines and small-scale gambling, neither of which she felt it necessary to give up after taking the veil. She got her revenge on her family's haughtiness in a way entirely in keeping with her character: she insisted on appearing at the coronation of her daughter-in-law, Queen Elizabeth II, in 1953, not in a bejewelled gown and tiara like practically everyone else, but in her grey nun's habit, which did, at least, make her recognisable in photographs. She returned to Greece to run her nunnery, but, perhaps unsurprisingly, the applicants struggled to meet her stringent entrance criteria and, in the end, the order numbered exactly one sister: Mother Superior Alice-Elizabeth herself.

Alice's spiritual quest took her further afield, not always with great success. A trip to India had to be cut short, to the ire of her hosts, when the nun-Princess began to have an out-of-body experience. As well as India, she also travelled to Rome, where Jacques, one of the Cohen sons who had escaped to Egypt, recognised her at an event. As he approached Alice to thank her for her bravery in hiding his family, she turned her beady eyes and famously sharp tongue on him. She told him she wanted no recognition – she had only done what her faith and her duty had compelled her to do.

Her life ended in the same way that much of it had been spent – in a strange mixture of pomp and poverty, a perfect elision of the sublime and the ridiculous. In April 1967, yet another military coup occurred in Greece and Alice, by now nearly as deaf as she had claimed to be in 1941, fled to stay with her son and daughter-in-law at Buckingham Palace. Despite her advanced age, she retained her nun's habit (and her smoking habit). As she wandered off down the long corridors of the palace, the servants were invariably able to trace her by the distinct trail of Woodbine smoke that accompanied her everywhere.

On 5th December 1969, Alice died, having given every last one of her possessions to charity. She left strict instructions that she should be buried, as was the popular Orthodox custom, on the Mount of Olives in Jerusalem, near the remains of the aunt who had so inspired her. When, as Alice lay dying, her youngest daughter Sophie complained that it would make visiting the grave very difficult, the nun-Princess narrowed her eyes for a last time and snapped, 'Nonsense! There's a perfectly good bus service.'

Despite her complaining, Sophie did manage to get to her mother's grave a number of times, including once with her brother Prince Philip in 1994, when, alongside the visit, they attended the World Holocaust Memorial Centre at Yad Vashem to witness their mother being honoured as 'Righteous Among the Nations' for her bravery during the war. Just as she had rejected praise from the Cohens in Rome, her son's quote at the time of the honouring could almost have come from the lips of Alice herself: 'I suspect that it never occurred to her that her action was in any way special. She was a person with a deep religious faith, and she would have considered it to be a perfectly natural human reaction to fellow beings in distress.'

Alice-Elizabeth, Princess of Greece and Denmark, was born to the mighty and their (admittedly regularly vacated) seats of power but spent her life 'exalting the humble and meek'. She was a great-granddaughter of an Empress, a grandmother of a King, a mother superior, a card player, an absent parent, a schizophrenic and a hero. If anyone embodies a Christian response to power, and in particular power misused against the weak, it is her.

— ARCHBISHOP DAMASKINOS OF ATHENS AND ALL GREECE —

'That scheming Prelate'

W hen His All Holiness, the Archbishop of Constantinople, New Rome and Ecumenical Patriarch, the nominal leader of the world's Orthodox Christians wants to enter his residence in the impressive St George's compound in Istanbul, he has to do so through a side door. The main gate, named for St Peter, has been welded shut since 1821. The reason for this seemingly self-defeating act of home improvement is that the site saw, on the Easter Sunday of that year, the judicial murder of the patriarch of today's predecessor, Grigorios V. Having celebrated the solemn Orthodox liturgy for Easter, Grigorios, still wearing his patriarchal vestments, was dragged from the cathedral on the orders of the Ottoman sultan Mahmud II, who was furious at his failure to suppress his fellow Greeks as they rebelled against Turkish rule. The Patriarch was taken to the gateway, where a rope had been looped over the lintel, and was there hanged. His death shocked and angered the Greek population, leading him to become a symbol of Greek refusal to give in to oppression. When Greek forces went into battle for their freedom (an enterprise in which they were, ultimately, successful), many of the soldiers carved the name 'Grigorios' on their swords.

In 1943, some one hundred and twenty-two years after Grigorios's execution, another figure of the Greek episcopate faced the very real threat of death at the hands of a furious foreign occupier. The committed Nazi general Jürgen Stroop, who, since his rather embarrassing dressing-down at the hands of Bishop von Galen of Münster in 1934, had risen to become the Head of the SS and Police service in Greece, was adamant that the Archbishop of Athens needed to be shot. Stroop had discovered that the prelate – Damaskinos Papandreou – in his role as both *de jure* religious and de facto political leader of Greece, had published a letter protesting the deportations of Jews from Thessaloniki to Poland. The letter contained the following paragraph:

According to the terms of the armistice, all Greek citizens, without distinction of race or religion, were to be treated equally by the Occupation Authorities ... In our national consciousness, all the children of Mother Greece are an insepa-rable unity: they are equal members of the national body irrespective of religion or dogmatic differences. Our Holy Religion does not recognize superior or inferior qualities based on race or religion, as it is stated: 'There is neither Jew nor Greek' (Gal. 3:28) and thus condemns any attempt to discrim-inate or create racial or religious differences.

Damaskinos sent the letter to the collaborationist Prime Minister but also ensured that it was disseminated as widely as possible, including having a copy delivered to Stroop's desk when he arrived in Athens in the September of that year. It is one of the only formal protests from a figure in authority that explicitly calls out the Nazi extermination of European Jewry. Stroop was livid and contacted Damaskinos, threatening to shoot him personally if he continued his advocacy for the Jews. With icy calm, Damaskinos composed a short reply to Stroop, which he, again, ensured was publicised. It read:

According to the traditions of the Greek Orthodox Church, our prelates are hanged; not shot. Please respect our traditions.

Stroop may not have fully appreciated the reference that the Archbishop was making, but the message was clear: the Greeks, and their Church leaders in particular, were not going to give in. Damaskinos's life was spared. Once again, the devout Nazi had been humiliated by a priest of a religion he viewed as weak and degenerate. Once again, an Archbishop had stirred up resistance among the people of Greece.

Where had Damaskinos got such courage? It might have had something to do with his upbringing. He was born Dimitrios Papandreou on 3rd March 1891, in Dorvitsia, a tiny village nestled among the mountain passes of the Aetolian region, Greece's Wild West. The people of Aetolia had a long-running reputation for being tough – ancient Greek historians considered their guttural pronunciation to be a sign of their semi-barbaric nature, as too was their insistence on eating all of their food raw. By the time of the future Archbishop's birth, cooking may well have reached the mountains of Aetolia, but many other comforts had not.

The Papandreou family were desperately poor, living a life of rural hardship dictated by the seasons and weather, in a manner not dissimilar to their grunting ancestors of yore. This was no barrier to Dimitrios, however, who showed himself to be both bright and ambitious.

By the time he was twenty-five, he had distinguished himself as a soldier during the Balkan Wars as well as read for degrees in both law and theology (the perfect combination of subjects, one might observe, to enable him to have an answer for everything). The following year, 1917, he was ordained, when, as was Orthodox practice, he took a new name, Damaskinos, as a mark of his devotion to the example of St John of Damascus (Johannes Damaskinos in Greek). John was a not an easy-going saint. He spent most of his public career as a thorn in the side of his rulers. Both the Christian Emperor and the Muslim Caliph conspired together to frame John for attempted treason, resulting in one of his hands being cut off, only for it to be miraculously restored as a sign of his innocence. He spent the rest of his days in a monastery, churning out letters and theological tracts designed to wind up those in power. It would be difficult to think of a more perfect patron saint for the prickly and precocious new priest.

The Aetolian's tough character was evident early on; not long after his ordination to the priesthood, the holy man was sent to sort out a most unholy row at the mountaintop monastery of Mount Athos. Three different national groupings had monasteries there, namely Greeks, Bulgarians and Serbians. They were doing what religious factions do best and falling out with each other in the most spectacular style, mostly about who took precedence over whom. Damaskinos arrived, banged their heads together and forced the warring monastics to sign a charter promising to behave in a way more befitting their calling. Such was his success at Athos that, barely five years after his ordination, Damaskinos was made a bishop, taking over the see of Corinth at the tender age of thirty-one.

His first trial as bishop was to come in 1928 when an earthquake struck Greece with Corinth at its epicentre. Although relatively few people died in the disaster, more than fifteen thousand were left homeless. The bishop leapt into action, organising a fundraising campaign for those affected. This was not, however, a case of upping the donations into the collection plate for the diocesan congregations; Damaskinos instead embarked on a global fundraising initiative, including a tour of America, all of which managed to raise the necessary funds. The American way of life had caught the young bishop's attention and he had seen the difficulties that the Greek community in the United States was having in maintaining its traditions. It was particularly unclear exactly who had religious jurisdiction over this burgeoning group of Orthodox faithful (over half a million Greeks arrived on the shores of the USA between 1890 and 1924). After a brief return to Greece, Damaskinos accepted a role as 'Exarch' of America, which, in practice, found him engaged in activities not dissimilar to those he had performed at Mount Athos. He arrived in New York in May 1930 and spent just under a year touring the country assessing what needed to be done. After a suitable number of heads had been knocked together and a new, competent leadership was installed, he returned to Greece in 1931. His reputation as Holy Orthodoxy's premier problem-solver meant that, after more successes in his diocese, on 5th November 1938 he was elected Archbishop of Athens and All Greece.

His election was controversial. On 4th August 1936, after an inconclusive election followed by months of political intrigue, Ioannis Metaxas, who had been sworn in as Prime Minister that April, launched a coup, supposedly to counteract planned industrial unrest. Metaxas banned political parties and gave himself the title of 'Leader of Greece' (though he also liked to be referred to by the bizarre title of 'First Peasant'). Greece's political landscape, which had never really been stable since the assassination of King George in 1913, was rocked again and a regime that used a number of the tropes of Fascism began to take shape. Metaxas, naturally, was adamant that there should be no opposition to his new regime, especially from the Church. He had wanted his candidate, a career diplomat named Chrysanthos, to be elected, but the Church's bishop-electors failed to play ball and selected Damaskinos instead.

Metaxas was furious and, after a month of wrangling, succeeded in getting the election overturned and Chrysanthos installed. Damaskinos refused to acknowledge Metaxas's jurisdiction over the Church and merrily continued to sign himself as Archbishop of Athens and All Greece on his correspondence. Metaxas, not a man renowned for his sense of humour or patience, became even angrier and exiled Damaskinos to the island of Salamis in the Aegean. Like a beardy episcopal Icarus, Damaskinos had flown high when young but had now crash-landed; doomed, it seemed, to spend the rest of his days looking out at the sea where so much Homeric heroism had been acted out, wondering why his chance to be a Greek legend had been so cruelly cut short.

†

It is a truism that we all make mistakes; acting in haste and repenting at leisure unites humans of all languages and cultures and is a trope repeated at every level – from individual errors to blunders by whole nation states. In April 1941, as the Germans finally managed to break Greek resistance and sweep into Athens, they made a mistake, which they, and their SS hero Jürgen Stroop, in particular, would come to bitterly regret. In early July, a figure made his way across the rocks and scrub that surround the Faneromeni Monastery on Salamis. It was a messenger from Athens come to inform the most high-profile of the monks there (and the only one there against his will) that he was once again Archbishop of Athens and All Greece. Chrysanthos's association with the government that had tried, albeit futilely, to resist Hitler and Mussolini made him unacceptable to the occupiers and so they allowed the Church to send word for Damaskinos to return as leader of the Church, working on the logic that he was their enemy's enemy. They were to discover just how flawed that logic was.

Damaskinos's full honorific included the title 'Archbishop of All Greece'. This was an aspect of his role that he took incredibly seriously; he did not consider himself to be (as the Nazis almost certainly did) some sort of Hellenistic Brahmin, concerned only with the maintenance of private worship for his own caste. On the contrary, Damaskinos believed that he was called to be the spiritual leader of all Greeks, regardless of whether they elected to attend Church. Indeed, with the absolute collapse of any other authority figure, he felt that his calling extended to being their effective political leader as well. Such an attitude set him on a collision course with the authorities. The Greece over which he was now indisputably Archbishop was in a desperate situation. The Axis occupiers were treating the country as a resource ripe for pillaging. They demanded extortionate contributions from farms and businesses in order to feed their armies and, by the autumn of 1941, famine had struck. By December 1941, the Red Cross estimated that nearly a thousand people were dying from hunger in Athens every day. The occupying forces continued to take what they needed and did practically nothing to assist the starving Greeks.

Damaskinos immediately set to work, calling on his old fundraising contacts in Britain, America and Turkey to help alleviate the ravaging hunger that was afflicting his compatriots. The fact that, by December 1941, Germany was at war with both the USA and Britain didn't deter him. Eventually, he and his fellow Orthodox bishops managed to get some food through to the general population, often arranging for supplies to be smuggled over the border with Greece's old enemy, Turkey.

As the Nazi campaign on the Eastern Front began to eat up more and more men, Berlin pressured the Greek collaborationist government to conscript men into military units to provide what was essentially slave labour for the mines, factories and farms that made the push towards Moscow possible. Throughout 1942 and into 1943, Damaskinos helped to coordinate and gave support to widespread strikes, which brought Athens to a standstill and convinced the Germans that a collaborationist regime that could barely police its own backyard would hardly be capable of furnishing the Wehrmacht with soldiers to defeat the USSR.

His actions in the strike and the famine earned Damaskinos the respect of the Greek people, both the devout and the less than godly, as well as the ire of the Germans, but it was, however, to be in 1943, when the Nazis set in motion the Holocaust in Greece, that Damaskinos's true hour of leadership was to come. His letter of March 1943, in which he quoted St Paul in stating that Jews and Greeks were one, had been prompted by the mass deportation of Jews in Thessaloniki, where both the city and the wider region were under German control.

The Nazi occupation saw the arrival on Greek soil of two figures particularly committed to the Final Solution. One was, of course, Jürgen Stroop, a man who, as we have seen, Damaskinos lost no time whatsoever in riling up. The other was Dieter Wisliceny, a hateful slab of a man who had only two masters: his stomach, and Adolf Eichmann, the architect of the extermination of European Jewry. At the end of September, Wisliceny ordered the Chief Rabbi of Greece to assemble a 'Judenrat' – a Jewish council – that was the inevitable precursor to deportations. By manipulating these councils, the Nazis routinely managed to squeeze money and resources out of Jewish communities with a promise of better treatment before deporting them to death camps anyway, with the inevitable excuse that the council itself was to blame for poor leadership. Chief Rabbi Barzilai was asked to form this council and to provide a full list of the members of the community in Athens. Having heard stories from the rest of Europe, he did no such thing, going instead to his old friend Archbishop Damaskinos for advice.

Damaskinos encouraged his Jewish friend to flee to the countryside, where resistance groups had managed to make the mountain passes and glades no-go areas for Nazi patrols, promising to do what he could. This the Rabbi did, burning all his documentation before he left. Damaskinos acted quickly; while Wisliceny pressured the Rabbi to form the Judenrat, Stroop had set 9th October as the day when the Jews of Athens had to report to the Nazis (perversely, it was the date of the Jewish feast of the atonement, Yom Kippur). The Archbishop called in another friend, the Athens police chief Angelos Evert, who was already treading a dangerous tightrope between maintaining contact with the government-in-exile and not getting shot. As the police chief entered nervously (the Archbishop was not exactly the person to be visiting if you were trying to maintain the illusion of neutrality), Damaskinos announced, in his booming voice, 'I have taken up my cross and spoken to the Lord; I have made up my mind to save as many Jewish souls as possible.' And so, with minimal discussion, it was decided; Damaskinos would instruct his priests to produce fake baptismal certificates, and Evert would instruct his officers to produce fake identification cards, all with the intention of providing cover for those whose lives were threatened by the Nazis. Over twenty-seven thousand such documents are thought to have been issued over the course of the following year.

As his letter showed, Damaskinos was not the man to limit himself to covert operations. Deep in his bones was a love for the drama of the Orthodox liturgy – this was a man who knew the value of a public display. He sent out a letter to clergy across Greece, insisting that they preach to their congregations on the absolute need to help one's neighbours. Orders went around the nation's monasteries and other religious houses to take in and hide Jews, especially children, if they came knocking. Damaskinos was determined that the Nazis would know exactly who was behind the efforts to defy the Führer's orders. This decision came with a great deal of risk – hundreds of clergy were arrested and executed for their efforts. It was not a decision that Damaskinos had taken lightly. That said, the chance to show up Stroop again may well have played a part in his course of action – he was almost daring the SS man to try and shoot him again. When Yom Kippur came, barely two hundred of the city's thousands of Jews turned up to register themselves. Once again, the great swooping figure in black had humiliated the zealous Nazi officer.

†

Across Greece, men and women looked to their Archbishop and followed his example. The island of Zante, now better known for acute adolescent alcohol poisoning than acts of heroism, became the place that was to carry out Damaskinos's order to the full. The island's mayor, one Lucas Carrer, was instructed to provide a list of the names and addresses of the two hundred and seventy-five Jews who lived there so that they could be rounded up and deported. The mayor was loath to do so and, being a good Orthodox believer, he went to the island's bishop, Metropolitan Chrysostomos. Inspired by his superior in Athens (and with that particular air that Orthodox clergy seem to have that, as one observer put it, 'God is standing directly behind them with a cocked revolver'), Chrysostomos took control of the situation. He immediately told Carrer to burn any documents that explicitly identified the island's Jews by their ethnic background before toddling down to the mayoral officer to reason with the German commander. The bishop rehearsed all the arguments that Damaskinos had made in his letter about the brotherhood of Jews and Greeks; all of which fell on deaf and unsympathetic ears. Exasperated, Chrysostomos grabbed a piece of paper from the desk, scrawled something onto it and thrust it into the hand of the SS officer. 'Here,' he said, 'is the list of Jews you required', and stormed out. When the paper was uncrumpled, it was revealed to have just two names on it: Lucas Carrer and Metropolitan Chrysostomos. The two proceeded to arrange hiding places for those at risk, playing dumb when the SS came calling. The Germans, frustrated at this show of Greek intractability, eventually gave up their hunt. Every single one of the island's Jews survived.

It was a similar story on the island of Volos, where Bishop Joachim and Rabbi Pesach conspired to hide over seven hundred Jews. When the bishop was questioned by the Nazis, he had only one answer, which he repeated whenever he was asked about the whereabouts of his fellow islanders: 'I am a Jew.' Damaskinos's message had finally got through, with hundreds of lives saved. The killings, however, continued, and, furious that the Archbishop had robbed them of prey, Stroop and Wisliceny finally had Damaskinos put under house arrest, and toyed with deporting him to a concentration camp. Even the problem-solver extraordinaire was only human in the scope of what he could do; by the time the Nazis, pressured by British and American advances in France and Russian advances in the east, finally evacuated Greece on 12th October 1944, over sixty thousand Jews had been murdered. In Thessaloniki, where evacuations had first taken place and where German control was tightest, nearly 90 per cent of the city's Jews died, with only one family in the entire city surviving the Holocaust without losing a single member. By contrast, in the rest of Greece, numbers, while still shocking, were much lower, due, in no small part, to the stand taken by the hardy cleric from Aetolia.

The end of Nazi occupation was not, however, the end of Damaskinos's time as a leader of his Church and people. The British arrived in Athens just two days after the German withdrawal, and a whole new stage of the struggle to shape the future of Greece began. Different partisans with wildly different political viewpoints (from Communists to reactionary monarchists) began to fight Allied forces and one another for control of the bruised and battered nation. With the King still in exile, the army obliterated and the democratic politicians in disgrace, it was clear that there was only one figure who could possibly unite the divided nation. Damaskinos accepted the title 'Regent' in an attempt to make it clear to the Greek people that his political powers were temporary (although he did, for a brief period in 1945, appoint himself Prime Minister as well, in an attempt to break a particularly intransient period of political deadlock). The great solver of problems was now in charge of the very sizeable problem that was post-war Greece.

You might have thought that his consistent anti-German stance throughout the war would have earned Damaskinos the affection of the Allies. However, tales of the Archbishop's ability to be pugnacious, prickly and downright pig-headed hadn't only reached Berlin and Rome, they'd made their way to London, Washington and Moscow too. Allied leaders resented having to deal with the man whom Churchill called 'a pestilent priest' and 'a relic from the Middle Ages' – they were trying to make a new world in the ruins of the old one and couldn't see a role for the guttural Aetolian utterances from the tall, bearded figure swathed in black. Inevitably, however, he earned their respect, with Churchill being the first to capitulate.

On Christmas Eve 1944, Churchill visited Athens in an attempt to coordinate the Allied response to the increasing hostilities that threatened to spill over into civil war. He stayed on HMS *Ajax* and invited Damaskinos aboard for talks. Prior to the Archbishop's arrival, Churchill had been full of vitriol about 'that scheming prelate, more interested in political power than the life hereafter'. However, after a couple of hours secluded with the cleric, even Britain's petulant prime ministerial bulldog was purring and addressing his Greek counterpart as 'Your Beatitude'. Diplomatic incident was avoided (although it came close when a group of sailors briefly mistook the Archbishop for one of their fellow mariners dressed up as a wizard for their Christmas fancy dress party) and so Damaskinos was left to rule Greece until the return of King George II. He spent his period in power desperately trying to calm tensions and find a peaceful solution to the civil war – particularly condemning the practice that had arisen among the partisans of kidnapping children as hostages. In 1946, he gave political power back to the newly returned King. By the end of May 1949, he was dead, having only just turned fifty-eight. Behind the cool façade and the quick tongue, the efforts of the war had left him broken in spirit and in health. Now that it was over, he was finally able to let go.

Winston Churchill was undoubtedly a man given to occasional hyperbole. His pre-meeting judgement of Damaskinos, however, does contain in it some truth. 'A scheming prelate, more interested in political power than the life hereafter' may seem harsh, but it's hard to think of Damaskinos himself as taking it as anything other than a compliment. Undoubtedly, he was a figure of great intelligence and, if that could be used to hoodwink (with an admirable panache) the blockheaded minions of a Fascist regime then it's difficult to blame him for doing so. The second part of Churchill's comment is, perhaps, the more interesting one. There are myriad theological opinions on how the here and now and the hereafter ought to interact, especially when it comes to what occurs in the political sphere. Damaskinos found himself embroiled in a situation where his choice to act politically was not a power grab by a crazed clericalist but the only intervention possible to save thousands of lives. His response to Stroop's threat was not just a spicy bon mot – he was aware of the effect the death of Grigorios had had over a century before and he knew that his actions were capable of inspiring just as much bravery from the people of Greece.

Damaskinos was a wily operator, a problem-solver, a fighter and a quick wit. But, above all, he was a man of a very profound faith, who believed in what he called 'the Holy religion'. That Holy religion informed him not to, in his own words, 'recognise superior or inferior qualities based on race or religion', and that is where Churchill's dichotomy was false – his interest in political power was entirely determined by his views on the life hereafter. To him, the saving of others was a matter of his own salvation as well. Damaskinos was nothing if not clear-headed – he knew what he needed to do to attain the heavenly life he professed belief in and, in his curt response to the ridiculous Stroop, he made perfectly clear which was his preferred way of getting there.

CALLED AWAY TO RESISTANCE

'They need me in these days of darkness'

I RELAND

— MONSIGNOR HUGH O'FLAHERTY —

The Scarlet Pimpernel of the Vatican

What have a would-be Irish golf pro turned priest, a ballad singer past her prime and the twelfth Duke of Leeds in common? They are not the start of a dirty joke, nor characters in a lesser known Mills & Boon novel (although, come to think of it, I haven't read them all). They were, in fact, the key players in one of the most impressive webs of espionage, trickery and heroism in the Second World War.

The Bible has rather a lot to say about the cause of the Gospel uniting the most disparate of figures – whether it be the irascible St Paul making common cause with the docile St Barnabas, or the boisterous Galilean St Philip becoming chums with an urbane eunuch from Ethiopia. Yet, even by the wacky standards of the New Testament, the group that came together in the *palazzi* on the northern side of the River Tiber were a very mixed bag, united by their conviction that something must be done to help those suffering at the hands of Fascism.

This ragtag group – for alongside performers and peers were myriad priests and nuns, a Maltese widow, a Swiss aristocrat, a madcap soldier with an instinct for survival and a roguish Cockney butler – was led by the Irish priest Monsignor Hugh O'Flaherty. He sat, spider-like, at the centre of a web of informants, refuges and disguises, relishing every opportunity he had to outwit the Gestapo. His is a story of daring escapes from stormtroopers, of late-night rendezvous and of cross-dressing clergy – all of it set on the stage of the Eternal City, a place where every paving slab has seen more drama and history than could fill any bodice-ripper paperback. Most of all, however, the story of Monsignor Hugh O'Flaherty is a story of redemption. How an angry partisan went from a narrow nationalism to an under-standing that God 'has no nation', of how a senior official of a Church, rightly criticised for not doing more to help the Jewish people of Europe in their darkest hour, risked his life doing exactly that. And, like all good stories of redemption, it is a tale of evil being thwarted and lives – thousands of lives – being saved. Unlike many stories of redemption, it is also a tale of false moustaches and nuns' knickers. So what *do* a would-be Irish golf pro turned priest, a past-her-prime ballad singer and the twelfth Duke of Leeds have in common? Redemption.

Amid the hills and inlets of Co. Kerry, on Ireland's south-westerly flank, nestled on the shores of Lough Leane, sits the Killarney Golf and Fishing Club, an august and venerable institution where the greens are as immaculately maintained today as when the club was founded in 1893. After about five years of the club's existence, the committee made the decision to employ a steward, one James O'Flaherty, who moved to the emerald valley from the comparative metropolis of Cork with his wife and children, including a newborn son named Hugh. Growing up in a world of balls and clubs naturally did wonders for young Hugh's handicap (he was a scratch golfer playing off zero by his mid-teens). The exaggerated stories that invariably accompany the post-game bar-side analysis must also have filtered through, as young Hugh became renowned for his anecdotes, delivered in a lilting Kerry brogue. However good his game (and it was said he might have made a living from it), he was no golf club bore, and his charm, quick wit and brains won him a scholarship to a teacher training college.

When Hugh was eighteen, however, his world was changed for ever by events that must have seemed a million miles away from the sleepy golf club on the shores of Lough Leane. The attempt by Irish republicans (with German support) to throw off British rule in the 1916 Easter Rising began a nearly eight-year period of internecine violence as the Irish fought the British and each other in a battle to forge an independent Irish state. Two years after the rising, in 1918, Hugh left golf behind and, to the surprise of many, also left teaching, and enrolled to become a missionary priest. Although prompted by a nascent sense of adventure, Hugh didn't get very far initially, ending up at a Jesuit training college just outside Limerick, a distance of little more than seventy miles. Meanwhile, as the 1920s began, the violent situation in Ireland grew worse. In the midst of these troubles, young Hugh lost friends in the particularly bloody fighting in the island's south-western corner as the green valleys of Co. Kerry became choked with smoke and blood. Hugh was very clear about the rights and wrongs of this particular conflict and, with all the fervour one would expect of a man in his early twenties, priestly training or no priestly training, would openly declare his hatred of Britain and all things British.

Indeed, when the violence in Ireland became too much and several seminarians, including Hugh, were moved over to the Collegio Urbano de Propaganda Fide (a training centre for missionaries) in Rome to finish their training, it was the British whom Hugh blamed. Despite his initial rancour at being made to leave Ireland for the first time in his life, Hugh flourished in Rome. His easy charm and razor-sharp intellect had caught the attention of his superiors and so the chippy golfer who had never left the province of Munster until a couple of years previously suddenly found himself in the Vatican's diplomatic service, representing the Pope in locations as far afield as Haiti, Egypt and Czechoslovakia. O'Flaherty rose steadily and, in 1934, was made a Papal chamberlain, which earned him the title of Monsignor and placed him near the heartbeat of the Roman Catholic political world.

And rather a murky world it was too. As the forces of Fascism began to rise across Europe, the Roman Catholic hierarchy were left in a quandary. On one side there was widespread fear of Communism among clergy and laity (given that the wholesale imprisonment and murder of religious believers was a key tenet of its programme). On the other there was the fact that Fascism was hardly pro-Christianity. Indeed, the founder of the movement was notorious anti-clericalist and probable occult sex fan Benito Mussolini. Having spent the period prior to the First World War writing unreadable anti-Catholic tracts, Mussolini's antipathy towards the Church mellowed somewhat when he started to smell power. Consequently, in 1929, he signed the Lateran Treaty with Pope Pius XI, a short-tempered mountaineering enthusiast from near Milan. The treaty established a temporal political entity over which the Pope could rule – Vatican

City – thus supposedly resolving the tensions between Church and state, but it also gave Mussolini exactly the sort of endorsement he needed for the gangster state he was constructing on the Italian peninsula. More problematically, it set a precedent for other concordats with equally dubious regimes (most notably with a Germany just a few years from a National Socialist takeover in 1933), making it look as if the Church was primarily concerned with protecting her own interests rather than condemning obvious wrongdoing. In 1939, the rambunctious mountaineering pontiff died, to be replaced by Cardinal Eugenio Pacelli, a Vatican career diplomat whose brother had negotiated the treaty with Mussolini and who had himself signed the agreement with Germany. The careful policy of the Church's top diplomats had seemingly received the endorsement of none other than the Holy Ghost.

Meanwhile, Monsignor Hugh O'Flaherty made himself available at parties hosted by ambassadors and ministers plenipotentiary to the Holy See, with one notable exception: the British. In fact, when war was declared by Britain on Nazi Germany in 1939, O'Flaherty, taking the official Vatican policy of neutrality to its absolute logical extreme, declared that, as far as he was concerned, 'there was nothing to choose between the British and the Germans'. The man who would be appointed a Commander of the British Empire at the war's end had quite the journey ahead of him.

†

Italy didn't declare war on Britain and France until 1940, and even that had only a limited impact on the Vatican diplomatic world and on the erstwhile Irish Monsignor. O'Flaherty did know that the British ambassador to the

Vatican, having been booted out of his spacious apartment in Italian Rome, was now holed up in a cramped office somewhere in the Vatican. The diplomat in question – the gloriously named Sir D'Arcy Osborne, heir to the Dukedom of Leeds – hadn't lived in such institutional conditions since his time at Haileybury. But he managed to make the best of it, maintaining an aristocratic charm that won round the paranoid Vatican staff, tetchy at the presence of an enemy of the Italian state. Osborne, and more especially his wheeler-dealer Cockney butler, John May, even elicited the odd courtesy from the arch-Anglophobe, Monsignor O'Flaherty.

Eventually, with the entry of the United States into the war in 1941, only one English-speaking diplomatic mission remained in Rome unhindered – that of the Irish Free State. The Irish diplomatic mission was under the direction of Dr Thomas Kiernan or, more accurately, that of his wife, the formidable Delia Murphy, a renowned singer, the zenith of whose career had been the release of a record entitled 'Three Lovely Lassies' by HMV. Murphy was increasingly disturbed about tales she had heard about the treatment of Allied prisoners of war, who, as the war progressed, were arriving in Italy in great numbers. Trapped by the need to maintain immunity and by the fact that many in Dublin made no secret of their desire to see Britain humiliated, even if that meant at the hands of the Nazis, there was little that Murphy could do. O'Flaherty, however, made extensive use of his diplomatic immunity to visit prisoner-of-war camps near Rome and gain as much information as he could about the soldiers held in them. Then, on return to the Holy See, he would ensure that the names of those he had traced were broadcast on Vatican Radio, a service which became a lifeline of hope for families in Ireland, and Britain, in despair at loved ones missing in action.

O'Flaherty's old passionate Anglophobia was giving way to compassion. It was a transition rooted in his own quietly but deeply held Christian faith; 'God,' he told his Irish critics, 'has no nation.' It was to become the motto that would guide him through the perilous period between 1943 and 1945. As the Allies invaded Sicily and Mussolini's government collapsed in the summer of 1943, Italy's minuscule monarch, Vittorio Emanuele III, ordered an immediate amnesty for prisoners of war. The rejoicing among the newly freed men was, however, short-lived, as the Wehrmacht ploughed across the Alps to install a new regime.

Ahead of the Nazis came a crowd of former prisoners, desperately seeking sanctuary in the neutral territory of the Vatican. Mindful of the fates of Bishop von Galen, Maximilian Kolbe and others, and petrified that the neutrality he had so carefully cultivated might be compromised, Pope Pius XII gave orders that Allied soldiers attempting to hide in or around the Vatican should be turned away. Monsignor Hugh O'Flaherty had other ideas. Many of the men remembered O'Flaherty's kindness during his prison camp visits and asked for him by name. Determined that, as 'God had no nation', it was as much his responsibility to save these men as anyone else's, the Monsignor, in defiance of Papal decree, Nazi diktat and, arguably, common sense, began to put feelers out to construct an elaborate escape network.

First, he recruited sympathetic figures in the Vatican to his cause – notably Delia Murphy, Sir D'Arcy Osborne and the even more marvellously named Swiss envoy, Count Sarsfield Salazar. The count and the ballad singer enjoyed Irish and Swiss diplomatic immunity and free movement, while Sir D'Arcy had links to British intelligence as well as, secreted around the tiny monastic cell that now represented His Britannic Majesty's Embassy to the Holy See, huge amounts of his own cash that he was more than happy to give to the project. Through his priestly contacts, O'Flaherty had also heard of a wild British officer running a network of escapees in the hill country just outside Rome. Major Sam Derry had been awarded the Military Cross for gallantry in North Africa, later escaping capture by launching himself headlong into a ravine. Recaptured, he escaped again while being transported through Italy and assumed command of a group of fugitive British soldiers. Using a series of disguises (including a cartload of potatoes), some bribes and playing on trusting Italian clericalism, O'Flaherty smuggled Major Derry into the Vatican, to a dinner party with none other than Sir D'Arcy Osborne (who was, for various reasons, disguised as a Monsignor). The real Monsignor and his ersatz English colleague invited the hardy Desert Rat to join them in a coordinating role in what they called 'the Rome escape line'. Derry accepted and so began O'Flaherty's career in espionage.

✝

The principle behind the Rome escape line was simple: hide as many people as possible from the Nazis and, therefore, save as many lives as possible. Achieving it was another matter, owing to the small difficulty of the Nazi occupation of Rome, which had occurred, with an accompanying declaration of harsh punishment for any who resisted, on 9th September 1943. Tasked with achieving the recapture of Allied prisoners and the rounding up of the city's sizeable Jewish population for deportation to Auschwitz was head of the Gestapo, *Obersturmbannführer* Herbert Kappler, the man who would play cat to O'Flaherty's mouse.

Almost immediately, Kappler informed the Jewish population of Rome that they might escape deportation if they provided him with a bribe of fifty kilograms of gold (equivalent to about £1.5 million today). O'Flaherty helped persuade Pope Pius to offer the sum to the Jewish community as an interest-free loan without a set repayment date – but in the end the Jews managed to come up with the sum themselves. The Jewish community, however, aware of Nazi double-crosses that had occurred across Europe, began to approach O'Flaherty in increasing numbers, asking whether they too might take advantage of the escape line. O'Flaherty now found himself at the head of an operation involving the clandestine and highly illegal movement of thousands of people, from Australian commandos to Italian-Jewish grandmothers.

O'Flaherty was not only the manager of the network – he was himself involved at the very front line of the missions and intrigue, taking him across Rome. It was O'Flaherty who sneaked across Rome in the dead of night to the flat of redoubtable Maltese widow Henrietta Chevalier and asked if she would take in escaped prisoners of war. It was O'Flaherty who rented the safe house on the Via Firenze, where Major Derry had first been secreted, and where countless others were hidden, and it was O'Flaherty who, when the Gestapo requisitioned the building opposite, laughed it off and reassured those hiding there, in his lilting Kerry drawl, that 'sure, they'll never look under their own noses'. (He was right.)

All this activity, however, soon came to the attention of Kappler. By observing the Vatican and through tracking down some prisoners hidden in religious houses, the Gestapo had deduced that a priest was responsible for their frustrating inability to track down Allied escapees and for the seeming disappearance of swathes of Rome's Jewish population. Kappler worked out that the Irish

Monsignor was the mastermind behind it all and decided that he would put a stop to the 'Scarlet Pimpernel of the Vatican', as O'Flaherty was becoming known, using force if necessary.

Ironically, it was Mussolini who indirectly saved O'Flaherty's life. While the Germans had occupied Rome, they were unable to occupy the sovereign and independent territory of the Holy See without enraging the sizeable Catholic population in Germany, as well as the few remaining neutral countries (such as Spain and the nations of South America) on whom they relied for economic and diplomatic links. So the Pimpernel was safe as long as he remained ensconced behind the colonnades of St Peter's. Kappler, aware that he couldn't touch O'Flaherty, wanted the priest to know that, as soon as he strayed into occupied Rome, there would be a price on his head.

One crisp autumn morning, a group of SS men arrived at the point where St Peter's Square meets the Via della Conciliazione. They were armed not with guns, but with pots of white paint. Priests and nuns watched on, bemused, as the crack troops of the Third Reich carefully marked out a long white line across the flagstones. This was no enforcement of parking regulations, nor an attempt at Fascist weather-proofing. It was intended as a sign to O'Flaherty – one that Kappler underlined by sending a message to the Monsignor's office informing him of the orders he'd given to the men who surrounded the Vatican compound: if the Irish priest crosses the line, shoot him. O'Flaherty was characteristically unfazed – indeed, over the course of the next few weeks, he ensured that he held each one of his meetings, often with contacts involved in the Rome escape line, on the steps of St Peter's Basilica, in full view of the German snipers on the other side of the white line.

With his identity revealed, O'Flaherty now had to watch his every move, but he didn't cease his involvement in the operation, nor his night-time forays into occupied territory. Kappler had developed a pathological hatred of the jovial Irish priest and now tried every trick in the book to eliminate him. He sent a group of heavies to try and jostle the clergyman over the fatal white line, to no avail. He dedicated large chunks of the military force defending Rome to surrounding locations which he believed O'Flaherty frequented, only to find that the Pimpernel had vanished into thin air. One reason the Monsignor appeared to have the powers of bilocation was that he had managed to get the tram and trolley bus drivers of Rome onto his side – saying private Masses for the devout drivers in return for concealment on a tram or bus as it trundled through the deserted streets with a 'not in service' sign clearly illuminated above it. The Pimpernel had managed to wangle his own private taxi service in the middle of one of the most closely watched and repressive cities on earth.

Under such circumstances, O'Flaherty's network of unlikely heroes became even more important. Delia Murphy started making increasingly regular trips in her husband's diplomatic car to less than salubrious locations across the city. This was no extramarital dalliance by a bored embassy wife – she was in fact using the vehicle as a makeshift ambulance to smuggle wounded prisoners of war and partisans to Vatican hospitals under the very noses of the Nazis. John May's web of illicit contacts in Rome's seedy underbelly became crucial to O'Flaherty's escapades, earning the Cockney rogue O'Flaherty's admiration, with the priest describing him as 'the most magnificent scrounger that ever lived'. Major Derry and his associate Lieutenant Simpson spent hours digging up parts of the Vatican gardens in order to find the biscuit tins filled with false documents that they had secreted there with O'Flaherty's blessing. At one point, threatened with discovery, they needed to effect a speedy costume change and the Monsignor, by now used to wearing a cassock, found himself short of a credible labourer disguise to lend and so gave Simpson the closest thing he had – his pair of lucky golfing trousers.

Changes of outfit became O'Flaherty's modus operandi. On one infamous occasion, he was visiting Prince Filippo Doria Pamphili, an urbane aristocrat with anti-Fascist sentiments, in order to collect a sizeable donation to the escape line. Kappler had watched O'Flaherty arrive and, as soon as he was upstairs, being entertained by the peer, surrounded the *palazzo* with Gestapo officers and ordered that the Monsignor be given up. In the panic, O'Flaherty ran down to the coal cellar, where, as luck would have it, the winter delivery was just being unloaded. O'Flaherty stripped down to his vest, threw his clothing in a sack, smeared coal dust on his face and made good his escape while Kappler's men stood by. On another occasion, he needed to make the journey across Rome on foot and, while the sight of a six-foot-two nun lumbering through the streets around the Vatican did elicit comment, O'Flaherty got away with it again. It wasn't only his own safety that he secured through disguise. Not long after the near-miss in the coal cellar, Kappler, infuriated that O'Flaherty had hoodwinked him once again, decided to arrest his collaborator Prince Doria instead. O'Flaherty got news of this and had the nobleman smuggled into the safety of the Vatican, dressed in the bright, distinct uniform of the Swiss Guard.

O'Flaherty's escapades were not, however, limited to these shows of priestly panache – every day he was engaged in the run-of-the-mill smuggling of individuals and families, with increasing numbers of Jews seeking safety. O'Flaherty would wait on his perch at the porch of St Peter's every evening and let it be known that those who needed help should come to him. In October 1943, aware that the status quo would not continue for much longer, an increasingly desperate Jewish couple came and begged the priest to hide their son, insisting he take a valuable gold chain as security. O'Flaherty went one better, disguising the couple themselves as a priest and a nun and giving the boy papers identifying him as an orphan. O'Flaherty then secured him a place in a Church-run hostel. When the couple returned to Rome, shaken but safe, after the war, O'Flaherty reunited them with their son and with their chain – which he had kept in his desk for the duration of the war, determined to return it to them.

By the time the infamous *razzia*, or round-up, of Rome's Jews occurred in late October 1943, of the nearly seven thousand still left in the city, the Nazis could only find a thousand and fifteen. O'Flaherty himself had helped persuade the paranoid Pope Pius XII that he had to open the Vatican to 'non-Aryans' at risk of deportation, which he did two days before the *razzia*, saving nearly five hundred lives. Yet the majority were already hidden in the monasteries, convents, presbyteries and Church properties that are around every Roman street corner. Many clergy were involved in the cover-up (notably the feisty French forger of passports Father Marie-Benoît, and, of course, the jovial martyr of the Esquiline Hill, Pietro Pappagallo), but the largest number owed their safety to the Pimpernel. By most estimates, he and his unlikely network hid nearly seven thousand people – whether Jewish, British, Polish, Italian or American.

Such bravery was not without a price. Five of O'Flaherty's associates were killed in the massacre at the Ardeatine Caves in March 1944. Others were captured, tortured and imprisoned. O'Flaherty himself used up more lives than a cat, such was the regularity of his brushes with capture. He was capable of making such a difference, undoubtedly, because of his high-ranking diplomatic position, but also, crucially because of his kindness and good humour. His network was so extensive because he was so persuasive, and he was so persuasive not because of clerical hauteur, but because of a disarming good humour combined with his simple, endearing faith in God (and a dash of elan).

During the height of his infamy, O'Flaherty was faced with a prisoner of war who would die if not operated on for appendicitis. Rather than give up on him, the Monsignor got the nuns at the San Spirito hospital (at this point requisitioned for German military purposes) to discreetly add the name of the man to the operating list. He was transported to his appointment in a diplomatic car secured through the aid of Delia Murphy and Sir D'Arcy and, when he arrived, was operated on by a German military surgeon and given time to recuperate in a ward full of Nazi officers, all at the expense of the Third Reich.

On another occasion, towards the end of the war, a German soldier who had collapsed in the street near the Irish delegation was brought to him by Delia Murphy, with the claim that he was, in fact, a priest, conscripted into the Wehrmacht, who had been fasting in an attempt to show contrition to God. O'Flaherty quizzed him and, when satisfied with his theological bona fides, accompanied the weakened man to the altar of the nearby chapel, and enabled him to celebrate Mass. As Delia Murphy watched, she was deeply moved not only by the moment of shared humanity but also, she wrote, by an awareness of the 'foolishness of war and the sacrifices of life'. Monsignor O'Flaherty had panache, a foolhardy bravery, but, above all, he had a deep love for his fellow man, regardless of what uniform they wore. Quite a journey for the angry and patriotic would-be golf pro from Killarney.

✝

On 5th June 1944, forces under the American Lieutenant General Mark W. Clark finally liberated Rome. Like all good commanders, Clark did a tour of the sights of the newly freed city, including, of course, the Vatican (which, for better or for worse, had actually been 'free' all along). Among those on the steps of St Peter's, he was introduced to a tall, mop-haired Irishman, who said simply, 'Welcome to Rome – is there anything I can do for you?' By anyone's standards, Monsignor Hugh O'Flaherty had already done plenty. He was, of course, showered with awards and medals for his heroism, including a medal from the British Empire, an irony given his past political enthusiasms. British or otherwise, O'Flaherty wasn't interested in medals, sending all of them to his sister back in Killarney to be kept in a drawer. In fact, at the end of the war, he famously remarked that the only thing he really wanted was the return of his lucky golfing trousers.

The motley crew that had run the Rome escape line disbanded, going on to lead their separate lives. Sam Derry secured a military promotion, but refused all other recognition. He was surprised (and not overly pleased) to appear in an episode of *This Is Your Life* in the early 1960s, where one of the guests who helped tell his tale was none other than Hugh O'Flaherty. Sir D'Arcy Osborne eventually inherited the title of Duke of Leeds but, preferring the weather, elected to remain in Rome, where he cut a debonair figure wandering idly through the city's streets. Delia Murphy continued to charm society wherever her husband was posted, meaning she ended up as the consort to the first ever Irish ambassador to Australia. John May, it will be of little surprise to learn, disappeared into thin air.

Herbert Kappler was arrested for the appalling crimes he enabled and committed in Rome during the Second World War. Sentenced to life imprisonment without parole, he was locked away in the military prison at Gaeta, just outside Rome. Such was the disgust at his actions that almost no one was prepared to visit him, with one exception: Monsignor Hugh O'Flaherty. Kappler was so impressed by O'Flaherty's desire to forgive that he converted to Catholicism, with the man he had spent several years trying to have shot administering the baptism. In 1977, a terminally ill Kappler managed to escape from military hospital by hiding in an enormous suitcase lugged in and out by his wife, ably assisted by two unwitting guards. He returned to Germany, where he died six months later. Perhaps it wasn't only Catholicism that he learned from O'Flaherty after all.

And what of the man himself? O'Flaherty remained in Rome for most of the fifties until, weakened by a stroke, he returned to the rolling green hills by the golf course at Killarney to live with his sister. It was there, where his adventure started, that he died in 1963. His life inspired countless books, a Hollywood film (*The Scarlet and the Black*, in which O'Flaherty was portrayed by none other than Gregory Peck), and also a stage play. The title is, of course, *God Has No Country*.

GREAT BRITAIN

— JANE HAINING —

The Sunshine Spinster

'How amiable are thy tabernacles, O Lord of Hosts' is a sentence found in Psalm 84. 'Tabernacle' isn't a word that pops up regularly in conversation. The original tabernacles were 'dwelling places of God' – places that the ancient Israelites specially set aside for their encounters with the power of the Divine. Yet, for all the lofty aims of the tabernacle, they were often more humble than you might imagine. Consisting of several layers of woven curtains draped round a series of poles, they were often little more than elaborate tents, designed to tempt the ethereal presence of the eternal Lord of Hosts to indulge in a spot of glamping. But so it was that the Hebrew people sought to encounter the ways of God – in an unlikely, makeshift structure on the rolling, sheep-scattered hillsides of Judea.

On a rolling, sheep-scattered hillside in Dumfriesshire, 'How amiable are thy tabernacles, O Lord of Hosts' are the words that a group of pious Scots Protestants chose to carve into the small chapel which they too had built in the hope of encountering the Divine. It was built in 1649, at the seemingly apocalyptic apogee of the English Civil Wars, when the presence of Divine power seemed both terrifyingly close and heartbreakingly distant. This little rock and brick tabernacle is perched on the hillside overlooking the small village of Dunscore. Nearly two hundred and fifty years after the chapel's construction, in a farmhouse just outside Dunscore, a baby was born to Thomas and Jane Haining, a couple who eked out a living farming the rolling, sheep-scattered hills around the tabernacle. The baby was given the same name as her mother: Jane.

She would grow up to join a select group of British subjects who chanced everything to save the lives of Jewish people in continental Europe during the Second World War, risking the double condemnation of being both enemy aliens and being complicit in helping the most despised group in Nazi Germany. It is a small and eclectic selection from the palette of English eccentricity – from the pair of opera-loving sisters who would use their fur coats to smuggle papers and money to the somewhat listless Anglican Vicar who ended up issuing certificates to aid the escape of hundreds of Viennese Jews. Haining, however, stands out among this motley crew for a number of reasons, perhaps the most striking and moving of which being that she ended her days a long way from the verdant valleys of Dumfries in the hell that was Auschwitz–Birkenau.

When Jane was just five years old, her mother died, leaving Thomas Haining to care for seven children. In the following years, Jane emerged from among the sizeable Haining brood as the child most likely to help her father with the rearing of her younger, and, at times, her elder, siblings. Being thrust into a world of proxy parenting and domestic work at such an early age did not, however, discourage Jane from entertaining dreams of a future beyond Dunscore. The family were deeply pious and, while other children whiled away the long hours of sermons in the little tabernacle kicking the backs of pews or planning adventures, Jane listened intently. She had a voracious appetite for books, with the little village school routinely having to source new volumes as Jane made short work of the entire contents of its little library.

After some cajoling by both the minister and the schoolmistress, both of whom had recognised Jane's talents, Thomas Haining was persuaded to allow his daughter to apply for a scholarship to the prestigious academy in the county town of Dumfries. The twelve-year-old Jane won it with ease and so, in 1909, set off with her satchelful of pored-over books on what must have felt like an astonishing adventure. This period fostered in Jane a lifelong love of education – especially, and unusually in the early years of the twentieth century, the education of women.

In Dumfries, she again impressed her teachers with her instinctive inquisitiveness, earning her the school's top prize. She had a natural ability and love for languages, her somewhat bookish demeanour transformed as she babbled away in proficient French and German. She soon earned a place at the College of the Glasgow Athenaeum, where she acquired the skills necessary to take a role as a commercial secretary (one of the new jobs opened to women after the profound sociological shift of the First World War). So, in the early 1920s, she joined the firm of J. & P. Coates Ltd in Paisley.

Yet work was not the centre-point around which Jane's life revolved. That was, and always would be, her faith. She worshipped in a soaring neo-Gothic church on the edge of Queen's Park in the south Glasgow neighbourhood of Govanhill. Ever curious, she was an avid attendee, not only of Sunday worship, but also the rigorous programme of 'improving' events that was often such an integral part of British Protestant denominations. For hundreds of thousands of Baptists, Methodists and Presbyterians, 'chapel' was so much more than a place for religious services – it was where wives met their husbands, families deposited their savings, and where many in the increasingly aspirant working classes sought an education. She attended as many talks and lectures as she possibly could, one of which, in the early 1930s, was given by the head of the Church of Scotland's mission in Budapest.

Jane was utterly transfixed. The thought of combining travel, work and faith in the service of others must have been especially appealing amid the belching chimneys of industrial Glasgow. Jane didn't have to wait long to follow her new dream. In 1932, an advertisement in a Presbyterian periodical caught her eye. It was for a post as a matron in a home run by the Scottish Church for destitute Jewish girls in Budapest. To Jane it must have seemed almost divinely ordained: all those years as de facto mother in Dunscore, all those hours spent with her nose deep in continental grammars and vocabulary books; they all pointed towards this. Needless to say, she got the job.

Budapest in 1932 was a great bustling conurbation at the crossroads of Europe. Its plum position on the Danube was at the geographical heart of *Mitteleuropa*, the half-imagined Habsburg hinterland between the excessive, fussy refinement of Western Europe and the brute force of the

Kievan Rus; between the clamour of Prussia and Poland to the north and the lazy, almost oriental, languor of the Balkans to the south. Its political situation, too, seemed to be stuck halfway between the old Europe of Kaisers and Tsars and the ideological dictatorships that now hemmed it in on every side. It was a monarchy without a King, ruled by the self-appointed regent Admiral Horthy, whom we met earlier, while its monarch lived in enforced exile. Finally, it was at the crossroads of the new ethnolinguistic nation states and the multi-ethnic empires of old. Budapest, in particular, was a conflation of every tongue and confession imaginable; home to Hungarians, Slovaks, Romanians, Germans, Roman Catholics, Calvinists and Orthodox. It was also home to nearly a quarter of a million Jews.

Indeed, the Jewish population was so large that the city was known in German as *Jüda-Pest*; over 60 per cent of the city's doctors and lawyers were Jewish. There were also substantial portions of the Jewish population eking out a living however they could, as tinkers, tailors, beggars or thieves. Judaism in Budapest had as many shades of synagogue as you could shake a stick at, but one thing that the diverse community had in common was an increasing uneasiness at the stories coming out of Germany. Horthy, in response to his pathological (but not unfounded) fear of the Soviet Union, cosied up to Hitler as a natural ally against Stalin, only increasing discontent among the Jews of Budapest.

It was in this febrile environment that Jane Haining arrived to take up her role as matron. Which seems a not unreasonable juncture at which to explain quite what the Church of Scotland was doing running a school on the Danube. During 1841, a group of Scottish missionaries had set out for Palestine in order to proselytise in Jerusalem.

Unfortunately, they never got as far as the great City of Zion as one of their number injured himself falling off a camel. A certain Scots scepticism descended on the venture and so the party returned home, by way of the Austro–Hungarian Empire. Stopping off in Budapest, they were astonished to find the city teeming with broad Scottish accents as the engineers shipped in from Lothian and Leith set about building bridges, tunnels and railways for the Austro–Hungarians. Convinced that this was providential, the group set up a mission to the workers, which eventually evolved into a church and school for poor girls, in the hope that the sway of the manse might keep them off the boulevards of Budapest. The school became incredibly well regarded, especially by the Jewish community, as it was less prescriptive about whom it would educate than the Empire itself.

And so to this strange corner of Dundee on the Danube came Jane Haining, determined to be as loving and motherly as she could to girls who were often rejected by what family they had on account of their sex and, increasingly, by society at large on account of their race. She was a natural. Jane genuinely loved the girls in her charge, taking care of their every need – from ensuring that they ate a hearty Scots-style breakfast of porridge oats each morning to arranging trips to the lakes of the Hungarian highlands, where she would boat, swim and play with her pupils as if she herself were eleven again. Of course, she kept her girls in line, but she was undoubtedly firm but fair – a Miss Jean Brodie figure transposed to an increasingly fraught *Mitteleuropa*.

Jane Haining, who had, even as a young woman in industrial Glasgow, made it a strict rule of life not to talk politics, was blissfully unaware of, one might even say stubbornly unengaged with, the escalating European crisis. She was in fact back in the United Kingdom, on holiday in the West

Country, when Britain declared war on Germany in 1939. Although Horthy's prevarication and backstage dealing meant that Hungary remained technically neutral, the elders of the Church of Scotland back in Edinburgh showed the same caution as their camel-riding forebears and ordered that the entire staff of the Budapest mission return (or in Haining's case remain) home. Haining ignored the warnings of both Church and state and immediately booked her return to Budapest, considering a looming world war only a minor inconvenience, and certainly not one that should prevent her from fulfilling her duty to her girls.

Over the following two years, Church officials repeatedly begged Haining to return, only for her to refuse every time. Ministers in Scotland became exasperated at her refusal to listen to reason, born out of a stubborn belief in the goodness of the people she was there to serve. In one of her many polite but firm replies to the Synod in Scotland, she wrote, 'These people are so true hearted and honourable that they will not harm a hair on my head.' In 1941, Horthy's delicate balancing act finally collapsed and Hungary declared war on the USSR, with Britain declaring war on the Hungarians in a gesture of support not long after. Jane Haining was now an enemy alien. Her Scottish colleagues sent one final plea to call the matron home. Haining replied with a typically respectful but curt letter, containing the words that were to become her epitaph: 'If these girls need me in times of sunshine,' she wrote, 'how much more do they need me in these times of darkness.'

†

Behind the somewhat austere façade of the schoolhouse in Budapest, the advent of war seemingly changed little.

By the cold January and February of 1942, the privation brought by wartime austerity had begun to bite, but that was nothing more than a jolly challenge for the resourceful matron. When, for instance, the soles of a number of girls' shoes began to wear out amidst the grey snow covering the boulevards, Haining cut up her leather suitcases for insoles to keep the girls' feet dry and warm. Food became harder to come by, but Haining managed the supplies in such a way as to make sure that the girls remained well fed. She even put together aid packages for British soldiers captured and interned near the Austrian border. She continued to tune in to the BBC most evenings; love Hungary though she did, some of the affectations of the strange group of islands in the North Atlantic inevitably remained.

For this blessed incubation from the mutual annihilation that was engulfing Europe, the pupils really had two people to thank. One was Jane Haining, who made sure to instil in them trust in and love for God and each with her oft-repeated maxim that not a hair on their heads would be harmed. The other, less likely, figure who shielded the girls of Budapest, was Admiral Miklós Horthy. The Hungarian regent's entry into the war had not especially affected his policy of prevarication. Hungarian troops were sent to the Eastern Front, including Horthy's own son, who died after a matter of days on the front line when his aircraft stalled just after take-off. But on a number of matters he resisted efforts by Berlin to influence domestic policy – in particular with regard to Hungary's Jews. He willingly allowed the deportation and mass execution of foreign Jews resident in Hungary (many of whom had fled there from the surrounding nations in the hope of sanctuary), as well as punitive measures limiting the number of Jews who could hold professional roles. When confronted with demands to send the entire population for Nazi 'resettlement', however, the Admiral sought to buy time by promising to do so incrementally. As a result of Horthy's non-committal attitude and the sacrifice of their foreign co-religionists, the Jews of Budapest – including the girls of the Church of Scotland school – were able to continue in the belief that they would be spared.

In early 1944, however, Horthy's (and by extension Haining's) luck ran out. Enraged by the Admiral's lacklustre attitude, Hitler ordered the invasion and occupation of Hungary. Horthy remained a pathetic puppet, but power was now increasingly in the hands of the Hungarian Arrow Cross movement. Within two weeks of German invasion, laws against foreign aliens were tightened and the entire Jewish population of Hungary – including Jane's girls – was put 'at the disposal of the Reich'. One day, some pupils came across their matron weeping as she darned their clothes, a task she normally took great delight in. On closer inspection they realised she wasn't darning at all but sewing child-sized yellow stars onto each of the girls' uniforms.

Haining's double identity as a known defender of Jews and as an enemy alien put her at obvious risk once the Nazis had taken full control of Hungary. In the end, it was the two most defining aspects of her ministry that led to her downfall: her implicit trust of the Hungarian people and her devotion to her girls. Not long after the German invasion, as food became even scarcer, Haining caught the son-in-law of the school's Hungarian cook stealing rations intended for the girls. Haining scolded him for putting his own needs above those of the pupils and assumed that would be the end of it. Within a couple of days, she had been denounced and the Gestapo were at the door. The horrors of war had finally come to the little Scottish school in Budapest.

The Gestapo provided a long list of Haining's supposed crimes, as detailed by their Hungarian informer: listening to the BBC, aiding enemy soldiers and, above all, working among Jews. During two hours of questioning, Haining, in perfect German, admitted to all of the charges except one. When accused of political activity, she vigorously denied it. Her intentions had never been political. She had only sought to do what she felt God had called her to do: to love the girls in her care. That very same morning, 25th April 1944, Jane Haining was arrested and taken away to prison.

But Jane had not left her girls unprepared. She, in cooperation with other staff, had helped a number of the students to escape Budapest, reaching contacts in the countryside and further afield. While officials were preoccupied with the arrest of their matron, there was a vital window for the staff and girls to smuggle those they could to safety. As the soldiers led her away, she turned back towards the crowd of scared girls who had gathered on the staircase and, with a smile, told them not to worry – 'I'll be back by lunch,' she said. It was the last time that the girls would see her, but some of them are still alive today.

Barely a month after her arrest, Jane Haining was shunted into a cattle truck at Budapest station and transported to Auschwitz–Birkenau. Ever since her arrest, there had been frantic attempts to free her by Bishop László Ravasz, the nation's pre-eminent Calvinist Church leader, but to no avail. Ravasz was put under house arrest for his trouble; the Nazis were determined to make an example of the farmer's daughter from Dumfries. Of course, she was not bundled onto the train to Poland alone. Such was the size of the Jewish population in Hungary and such was the efficiency of the Nazi killing machine that it is estimated that in May and June 1944 some twelve thousand people a day were transported to death camps. Doctors and lawyers were thrown in with the tinkers and tailors, and in among them all was

Jane Haining. Conditions on the trains were appalling and the treatment of those deported truly shocking. Families were split up, leaving many children terrified. Jane, aware of the calling she had left behind, did what she could, with a particular eye for girls separated from their mothers. A word of comfort here, a held hand there. Some sunshine amid the darkness.

On arrival at the train station at Auschwitz, all those designated fit for slave labour were tattooed with a number to render them identifiable as prisoners, even when the extreme privation in the camp rendered them barely recognisable as humans. Jane Haining's number was 79467. On 15th July 1944, Haining somehow – perhaps due to her conspicuous non-Jewish status and her British rather than Hungarian citizenship, perhaps just due to her stubborn persistence – managed to get a final letter to her colleague and friend, Miss Prem, back in Budapest. The scrawled German contains no reference to her own state, only concerns about the welfare of the girls and lines of affection for Miss Prem. Her one reference to herself is to say that she is 'on the way to Heaven'. Even as she suffered under the most egregious example of man's inhumanity to man, she kept her humanity. When God might have seemed dead amid the horrors of life on earth, she kept her faith in a better life beyond.

On 17th July 1944, Jane Haining was recorded as having died of inflammation of the intestine. It is almost certain that, in fact, she was gassed to death with a group of women from Hungary in the chambers at Birkenau the day before. She died with those whom she had felt called to serve in life – the forgotten, then despised, Jewish women of Hungary.

Tens of thousands of years since the Israelites sought the comfort of God's presence in those tabernacles on the parched hillsides of Judea, a woman from the hill country of Scotland sought to make the presence of God known in the best way she knew how; by showing love to her fellow humans despite the most appalling of circumstances. On the slopes above Dunscore, just outside that other ramshackle rock tabernacle with the words of the psalm carved on its side, a small memorial bears the name and briefly tells the story of Jane Haining. Her name is now inscribed not only on the windswept hillside near Dumfries, but also on a hillside overlooking Jerusalem, not far from where those first tabernacles were constructed. She is listed as one of the 'Righteous Among the Nations' at the World Holocaust Memorial Centre of Yad Vashem.

'How amiable are thy tabernacles, O Lord of Hosts.' If a bedraggled tent on the Judean hillside was an unlikely place to see the power of God in action, how much more so is a converted cattle truck or an uninhabitable barrack hut on those bare Polish plains. Yet the life and witness of Jane Haining is testament to just that; so too was her death. Sometimes the most powerful stories aren't those that end with triumph, or are replete with bombs and bombast. Sometimes resistance doesn't take the form of an inspired speech or a great public deed. Sometimes the most powerful moments are found in the most unexpected and unlikely places. Sometimes resistance is saying you'll be back by lunch. Sometimes it is holding a frightened little girl's hand.

RESISTANCE AFTER 1945

'The King's table'

THE UNITED STATES OF AMERICA

— PASTOR FRED SHUTTLESWORTH —

Not Raised to Run

O ne of the most popular songs of the Christmas season of 1956 was a rendition of 'I Heard the Bells on Christmas Day' sung by Bing Crosby. It was played on record players in comfortable stuccoed living rooms across Middle America – the soundtrack to the chocolate-box Christmases of which the Janets and Johns of the world's new superpower had long dreamed. Yet, while Bing's beguiling baritone gave the song a jovial and festive air, the lyrics (in fact a poem written by master of American folk gloom, Henry Wadsworth Longfellow, at the height of the American Civil War) painted a much darker picture than many of its listeners may have realised:

> I heard the bells on Christmas Day
> Their old, familiar carols play
> And wild and sweet

The words repeat
Of peace on earth, good-will to men!

...

And in despair I bowed my head;
'There is no peace on earth,' I said;
'For hate is strong,
And mocks the song
Of peace on earth, good-will to men!'

The Christmas of 1956 was a long time after the American Civil War (indeed, the last surviving veteran of the conflict had died in the August of that year) and yet its scars still remained. Hate was still strong in the Deep South.

The Advent period had been busy for the Reverend Fred Shuttlesworth, Pastor of Bethel Church, a Baptist congregation in Birmingham, Alabama. Any cleric of any denomination will be only too happy to relate the litany of services and events that they have to attend at that time of year. Fred Shuttlesworth had not only the normal round of carol services, Bible studies and Christmas visits that the festive season brings to clergy; he spent every spare hour he had involved in the civil rights campaign, chairing the Alabama Christian Movement for Human Rights, founded by Shuttlesworth in May that year when the government of the state closed down other anti-segregation organisations formed by the National Association for the Advancement of Colored People.

With a dual career as pastor and politician, it was no surprise that, on Christmas night 1956, Fred Shuttlesworth had gone to bed early. Not long after 9 p.m., the parsonage where Shuttlesworth and his family lived was ripped apart by an explosion as sixteen sticks of dynamite detonated the other side of the pastor's bedroom wall. They had been planted there by the Ku Klux Klan, determined to kill Shuttlesworth and, in so doing, teach others a lesson: that the segregated system, whereby black people were denied their rights through both institutional racism and vigilante action, was not to be messed with. The whole neighbourhood heard the explosion and, in nightdresses and dressing gowns, burst out onto the street, expecting to find their pastor lying dead in the cold Christmas air. In fact, miraculously, Shuttlesworth had survived, having fallen through the collapsed floor of his bedroom into the basement, where he was found by police under a mound of rubble.

Shuttlesworth's first instinct was to go and reassure his neighbours and congregants that there was no danger to them. He was a committed advocate of non-violent resistance to the system of segregation and was determined that the attack on him not be mobilised to stoke up tension or incite violence. As he went towards the assembled crowd, a police officer, himself a member of the Ku Klux Klan, came up to Shuttlesworth and, disguising a clear threat under the sheep's clothing of friendly advice, warned the pastor that 'if I were you I'd get out of town as quick as I could'. Shuttlesworth turned, looked the man squarely in the face and replied, 'I wasn't raised to run.'

†

Fred Shuttlesworth wasn't raised to run. He was raised on a small, subsistence farm near the unincorporated settlement of Mount Meigs, Alabama – a place famed only for the looming presence of a large juvenile correction facility, the gruesomely named 'Alabama Reform School for

Juvenile Negro Law-Breakers'. He was born, out of wedlock, to Alberta Robinson and one Vetta Green in 1922. Fred would be brought up, however, with his stepfather, William Shuttlesworth. William was a farmer who scraped a living from the cracked, dusty earth around Mount Meigs and so endeavoured to feed his eight children and, of course, his stepson. Young Fred grew up in desperate poverty (a fact that would set him apart from other leaders of the civil rights movement such as Martin Luther King, the pastor's son who was to become Shuttlesworth's friend, ally and sometime rival). He worked a series of manual jobs, regularly finding himself driving vast trucks along the state highways, in his teens and twenties, but, with a devout faith, he eventually earned a place to study at a seminary in Selma, where, during his training, he gained a reputation as a fiery and fearless preacher.

From Selma, the young pastor was sent to Birmingham, Alabama, to take up the leadership of First Bethel Baptist Church in 1953. Birmingham had been founded after the American Civil War in an attempt to create a centre for a new Southern industrial economy and so wean Dixie off her dependence on agriculture, which was itself, in turn, dependent on slave labour. Growth was initially explosive, earning Birmingham the nickname of 'The Magic City'. However, it was, in the words of President Franklin D. Roosevelt, 'the worst hit town in America' by the effects of the Great Depression. Work became scarce, people became resentful and racial tensions bubbled over. By the fifties and sixties, Birmingham had become explosive for another reason. It earned a new nickname – Bombingham – as the Ku Klux Klan smuggled dynamite and explosives from the city's industrial areas to wage a campaign of terror against black communities. And so it was to Bethel – not in the Holy

Land but in Birmingham – that young Fred Shuttlesworth came to spread the Gospel.

It did not take long for Shuttlesworth to preach politics. Almost all the leaders of the civil rights movement – men such as Martin Luther King, Jesse Jackson or Ralph Abernethy – began their careers as clergy. The fierce commitment to their flock's common humanity in the face of daily indignities and violence meant that it was the clergy who were first to speak out. These men did not hold to the secularist mantra that politics and faith ought not to mix. Rather, they became active in marches, boycotts, votes and agitation for justice – and Fred Shuttlesworth was to become the cleric-activist par excellence.

Shuttlesworth had joined the National Association of Colored People not long after arriving in Birmingham in 1953. When it was outlawed from operating in the state of Alabama, he became active in its replacement, the Alabama Christian Movement for Civil Rights, a move which resulted in the bombing that Christmas night in 1956. Shuttlesworth, whom Martin Luther King was to describe as 'the most courageous Civil Rights fighter in the South', wasn't going to give up, and so, a year later, he, King and a group of other activists and clergy founded the Southern Christian Leadership Conference. The group had non-violence and passive resistance at the very heart of its mission statement. Shuttlesworth, who had been adamant that the Christmas bombing not be used to inflame tensions, would soon be given another opportunity to show his utter commitment to this radically non-violent creed.

On 9th September 1957, at the start of the new school year, Fred Shuttlesworth and his wife Ruby took his two daughters, Patricia and Ruby, to be enrolled in Phillips High School in downtown Birmingham. Parents across the city were doing the same thing; Phillips was a prestigious school, renowned for its good grades. It was also all-white. When Shuttlesworth and his family arrived at the school and tried to gain entry, they were set upon by a mob of Klansmen. Shuttlesworth was whipped, beaten with brass knuckles and lashed with bicycle chains. His wife was stabbed. The police were nowhere to be seen. A bruised and beaten Shuttlesworth managed to get his wife back into his car, where, still bleeding, he drove them both to hospital. On the way there, he preached an extempore sermon on the need for perfect and complete forgiveness to his children, who were still sitting, shaken, in the back seat. When he arrived at the hospital, the doctor who treated him expressed amazement at the fact that Shuttlesworth had not suffered a serious concussion. The pastor nonchalantly replied, 'Well, doctor, the Good Lord knew I lived in a hard town, so he gave me a hard head.' Very few men would have forgiven such an act. Even fewer would have stayed and doubled down on their efforts; many would have remained angry, more would have run. But, as we now know, Fred Shuttlesworth wasn't raised to run.

Shuttlesworth's willingness to forgive as part of a commitment to overturning segregation did not, however, nullify his naturally combative streak. His language, in stark contrast to King's classically constructed oratory, was blunt and earthy. He stated his aims in activism simply: 'I mean to either kill segregation, or be killed by it.' Sometimes his confrontations were not with the Birmingham City police or the Klan but with his own colleagues, resulting in even more colourful language. He once exploded at King, who had gone behind Shuttlesworth's back (as he saw it) to negotiate with shopkeepers in Birmingham, telling him 'you're Mister Big, but you're going to be Mister S-H-I-T'. He would routinely vent his frustration at King's use of 'flowery speeches,' while Shuttlesworth spent time on the ground, regularly getting injured and thrown into prison. Yet, for all his confrontation, he acknowledged King's contribution and the key role his leadership played, and, after King's assassination in 1968, mourned his death. For all his criticism of King, Shuttlesworth was perfectly capable of playing the politician as well – it was he who, after five years of hounding, eventually persuaded King (and the global media that followed him) to come to Birmingham in 1963 for a series of demonstrations that would change the course of American history.

It was said that he took his survival on Christmas Day 1956 to be a sign from Heaven that his mission was blessed and no harm would come to him. That conviction made him an inspiring figure in a movement that seemed to be flying in the face of intractable opposition. Shuttlesworth had a habit of walking, calmly and confidently, through crowds of pro-segregation agitators, their faces purple with hate. 'He was either insane or the most courageous man I have ever met', as James Farmer, another prominent civil rights leader, put it. Whether it was courage, insanity or a devout faith that inspired Shuttlesworth, one thing is sure: he believed in civil rights and would neither give up nor sell out. Unfortunately for the Reverend Fred Shuttlesworth, the man who was to become his nemesis felt exactly the same way about segregation.

The fate of the Reverend Fred Shuttlesworth was inexorably bound up with that of Theophilus Eugene 'Bull' Connor. Connor had first been elected to the post of Commissioner for Public Safety in Birmingham in 1936 and, with a short hiatus between 1952 and 1957 to embark on a disastrous campaign for the role of state Governor (with his primary policy being to 'outlaw' Communism), he would remain in that post until 1963. His comeback as Commissioner was on the back of a promise to deal with the increasing anti-segregationist agitation. Connor came to loathe Shuttlesworth, routinely raiding his parsonage, having him arrested on any charges he could concoct (including vagrancy, which meant he could keep him in prison without offering bail) and instructing his officers to use increasingly violent means to deal with the protests.

Shuttlesworth spent the years 1960–62 testing the notoriously irascible Connor's patience to the extreme by participating in a series of sit-ins at segregated diners across Alabama (which invariably involved Shuttlesworth and his fellow protestors being showered with mustard, milkshakes, fries and phlegm by the patrons). Shuttlesworth also played a central role in organising the Freedom Rides of 1961, where a number of activists from northern states were bussed into the South to support efforts against segregation there. Shuttlesworth used every available space at the parsonage to host the freedom riders and, when a group were ambushed and their bus firebombed by a Klan-sponsored mob at Anniston, Alabama, Shuttlesworth organised a rescue convoy of fifteen cars to whisk the riders away from the very real prospect of being lynched. Later, when a group was surrounded by an angry mob in Birmingham itself, Shuttlesworth appeared and, like a latter-day Moses parting the Red Sea, glided through the crowd with an air that was, in the words of one contemporary, 'as cool as a cucumber'. Connor was livid at Shuttlesworth's involvement with these events – all of which put the national spotlight on how black people were treated in Alabama. But Shuttlesworth wasn't done. In 1963, he put forward 'Project C' to his fellow civil rights leaders: 'C' for 'Confrontation'. They were going to escalate the campaign to show the ugly underbelly of racist America not just to the nation but to the world.

After arranging for King to join the protests in Birmingham, Shuttlesworth set about mobilising the forces of his Alabama Christian Movement for Human Rights to engage in protests across the city in April and May. Connor immediately took the bait; he deployed attack dogs to savage protestors, fire hoses to blast them back and liaised with the Klan in an attempt to crush Shuttlesworth once and for all. King arrived in Birmingham in early April and, on the 12th (Good Friday), he and scores of others were arrested. By 3rd May, things had come to a head – not least as Birmingham's prisons were now full. On 7th May, Shuttlesworth mobilised a group of around two thousand young people and students to march through Birmingham in a 'Children's Crusade', demanding an end to segregated institutions and businesses. Shuttlesworth was playing in an incredibly high-risk game. Would Bull take the bait and show the city up to be the sort of place that used force against children? And, if he did, was the pastor gambling with innocent lives?

In the end, Connor fell for Shuttlesworth's gambit. He deployed dogs, armed police and water cannons on the protestors. A number were injured, but none were killed. Among those hurt was Shuttlesworth himself, who suffered the full force of a water cannon as it propelled him into a brick wall and caused multiple chest injuries. Shuttlesworth was rushed to hospital. When Bull Connor was informed of the incident, he remarked, 'I'm sorry to have missed it – I only wish they'd carried him away in a hearse.' But the only fatality that day was to be Bull Connor's career. The photographers and journalists who had followed King down to Alabama documented the astonishing brutality of Connor and his men. Pictures of students being knocked to the floor by hoses, clergymen being beaten by batons, schoolchildren being savaged by dogs made front-page news across America and around the world. Editorials howled at the horrors they saw, President Kennedy publicly declaring that the pictures made him 'feel sick'.

Birmingham's leaders backed down. Connor was sacked and, in September that year, the city's schools were integrated. When President Kennedy himself embraced the cause of civil rights in June 1963, he commented that, without Birmingham, none of his proposed changes would have been possible. He might as well have said 'without Fred Shuttlesworth'.

However, the struggle for civil rights was nowhere near over. King and Shuttlesworth continued to fight to ensure that rights for black people became more than a dream. Crucial to this was the famous marches from Selma to Montgomery in 1965 – as one contemporary put it, 'If Birmingham killed segregation, then it was Selma that buried it.' Shuttlesworth was there over the course of the marches, including on Bloody Sunday when the marchers attempted to cross the Edmund Pettus Bridge. There, a large group of clergy from all over the country led the crowd in a peaceful procession, only to be met by batons and tear gas. Shuttleworth stood a couple of places along from King himself, linking arms with a prominent Rabbi and the Greek Orthodox Archbishop in America, his fiery Baptist background put aside in a moment of interfaith solidarity. The clerical leadership meant nothing to the Alabama police – one white minister, there in solidarity, the Reverend James Reeb, was beaten so badly that he died.

Like Birmingham, Selma shocked the nation and led President Lyndon B. Johnson to sign the Voting Rights Act into law, ensuring that the legal loopholes with which the states of the Deep South had denied their black citizens their most basic rights were closed. Again, Shuttlesworth had played a crucial part in the clerical crusade to ensure that racism was banished in a wider vision of the supposed American Jerusalem. Yet, as we know, Selma was not the end. Martin Luther King was murdered three years later. After so many years dedicated to political struggle, Shuttlesworth returned to preaching and pastoring, founding a new congregation in the Greater New Light Baptist Church in 1966. His childhood meant that he was intensely aware that political oppression had gone hand in hand with material poverty and economic abandonment for many black people in the South and so, in the 1980s, he founded the Shuttlesworth Housing Foundation, designed to tackle the blight of homelessness and poor housing in his community.

'That Fred Shuttlesworth did not become a martyr was not for lack of trying.' So wrote the pugnacious pastor's biographer as his subject transitioned from 'The Wild Man of Alabama' to elder statesman of the civil rights movement. It was somewhat ironic that Shuttlesworth, a man who deliberately put himself in the way of bricks, bone-breaking hose blasts and bombs, should outlive almost all the other leaders of the anti-segregation movement. But outlive them he did, even surviving to see the main airport of Birmingham, Alabama, renamed Birmingham-Shuttlesworth International in May 2008. He lived until

2011, meaning he saw the election, in November 2008, of the first black president of the United States. Shuttlesworth knew as well as anyone how much further that nation had (and arguably still has) to go, but he, more than many, died knowing how far things had come, due in no small part to his life and ministry.

In Birmingham, Fred Shuttlesworth ploughed a furrow that others told him was foolish, that flew in the face of authority. Violence by the Klan couldn't stop him, threats by Bull Connor couldn't stop him, advice from his nearest allies couldn't stop him. And so it was that he helped bring Dr King's famous dream a little closer to reality. Through the sheer bloody-mindedness of Fred Shuttlesworth, hope faced down fear.

After he died, the flags on Alabama state buildings (including places where Shuttlesworth had protested, stood trial and been imprisoned) were lowered to half-mast. That the heart of the old Confederacy could honour a poor black preacher man in such a way would have seemed unthinkable in Mount Meigs all those years ago, but, in part due to his dogged determination, Birmingham, the state, the country and the world that Fred Shuttlesworth grew up in was very different from the one he left. He forced the world to change because he wasn't going to give any ground. After all, he wasn't raised to run.

— SEMINARIAN JONATHAN DANIELS —

Martinis, Martyrdom & a Missed Bus

For all the narrative of the anglophone West being a post-Christian culture, there are still many phrases that have their origins in the Bible. For instance, a reference to 'the writing on the wall' is drawn directly from an incident in the Book of Daniel where ominous graffiti ruins a dinner party. Meanwhile, the exhortation to 'eat, drink, and be merry, for tomorrow we die' is not originally from Shakespeare or even Hollywood but, rather, is found in a number of places across the Bible, most notably in the Book of the Prophet Isaiah.

One of these biblical hangovers in the Western collective lexicon that still sends shivers down the spine is spoken by Jesus in the Gospel according to St John: 'Greater love hath no man than this, that he lay down his life for his friends.' It is etched on war memorials across the English-speaking world and invokes an ideal of self-sacrifice of the very loftiest sort. For most people, Christians included, it is a maxim that will never be put into practice, remaining a lofty ideal or a stock phrase deployed at apposite moments. (Or twisted – one politician famously quipped during a brutal cabinet reshuffle that 'greater love hath no man than this, that he lay down his friends for his life'.) However, Jonathan Daniels, a trainee Anglican priest in the United States during the troubled years of the mid-twentieth century, did lay down his life in a tragic, brave flash one hot and hazy day in August 1965. Martin Luther King referred to the circumstances of his death as 'one of the most heroic Christian deeds of which I have heard in my entire ministry'.

Jonathan Daniels was an unlikely hero in a number of ways, not least as a privileged Northern white man in the context of the struggle for civil rights in the Deep South. Yet such was his commitment to bridging divides, to denying a narrative of hate, to his friends, regardless of the colour of their skin, that he laid down his life. For Jonathan Daniels, those words in the Gospel according to St John were not just a lofty ideal, they were the reality around which he centred his life, and, on a stifling afternoon in Alabama, his death as well.

The history of the Church is full of unlikely saints, but Jonathan Daniels' upbringing was not one you would expect to lead naturally to his becoming an icon of Christian justice. Contemporary politics on the Western side of the Atlantic has been much exercised about the existence of 'Two Americas', two nations that exist side by side and yet know and understand nothing of one another. Jonathan Daniels, born in the leafy, prosperous small town of Keene, New Hampshire, and killed in the dank and dusty streets of Hayneville, Alabama, took the unusual step of trying to reach one America from another.

His parents were prosperous professionals – a consultant physician and a languages teacher who were observant

Congregationalists. However, exhibiting the respect for individual choice for which their mountainous little state (motto: 'Live Free or Die') was famous, they allowed their second child, Jonathan, to attend the Episcopal Church to which his scout group was attached. It was during his time at high school that the naturally inquisitive and adventurous Jonathan suffered a relatively serious fall from a roof during a night-time escapade, putting him in hospital for a month. During that month of November 1955, the hours of reflection made him turn to prayer and consideration of his own future and so he left his sickbed resolved that he was called to be an ordained minister in the Church. However, he was first sent to the Virginia Military Institute, a prestigious military school known as 'The West Point of the South'. During his time there, the death of Daniels' father profoundly challenged his faith and, for a while, he put his dreams of ordination on hold, instead throwing himself into his military studies. He graduated valedictorian of his class in 1961, giving an inspiring speech to his fellow classmates. Yet a military career was not to be; Daniels had also thrown himself into his academic work while in Virginia and so, in the autumn of 1961, went back north to enrol as a student at Harvard University, with the intention of majoring in English Literature. At some point between 16th and 22nd April 1962, Holy Week, Daniels, who had dragged himself along to the Church of Advent in Boston, perhaps more out of duty than in expectation of reconversion, underwent a profound religious experience (the details of which he, in a reticence unusual for one so sociable, never shared with anyone) that left him convinced that the priesthood was his calling.

†

The Episcopal Church was (and in many ways still is) a somewhat strange ecclesial body, balancing two very conflicting identities. On the one hand, it is a part of the Anglican Communion, which provides a tangible link back to England, America's old foe, and her historic Church, which so many of the continent's early settlers were determined to escape. Yet, on the other, the Church was founded in direct defiance of orders from Canterbury, making use of rogue Scottish bishops to ordain their first clergy. On one hand, it became the Church of America's elite, producing more presidents from its pews than any other denomination, as well as feeding the souls of countless Vanderbilts, Astors and Morgans over the centuries. On the other, it has become famous for taking the social mission of the Gospel seriously, opposing the death penalty and advocating for issues such as the minimum wage and gay rights in the face of opposition from many in American society. It occupies a strange place in American religious and social culture that was, perhaps, best summed up by the late comic actor Robin Williams (himself a committed Episcopalian) as 'Catholic Lite – same religion, half the guilt'. It was to this Church, with its fiery commitment to social justice under a cloak of establishment gentility, that Jonathan Daniels decided (after much trepidation, uncertainty and a loss of faith) to enter as a seminarian.

In the autumn of 1963, Daniels left Harvard and enrolled at the Episcopal Theological School in Cambridge, Massachusetts. He was considered a model student: erudite without being awkward, curious but obedient. Such was his commitment to his studies and to the rules that, when Dr Martin Luther King made his appeal to his fellow religious leaders to come to Selma, Alabama, to protest against the treatment of black people in the state, Daniels initially declined to join fellow seminarians who were determined to go. This was in part due to his commitment to his books but also to the fact that the elderly and cautious Bishop Carpenter, head of the Episcopal diocese of Alabama, aware of the particular reputation that his Church had of supporting 'outsiders' or Yankee 'carpetbaggers', had asked clergy from the North to stay away.

Not long after that, Daniels recalled being at Evening Prayer in the college chapel when a second life-changing incident occurred. At the heart of the Anglican service of Evensong is the Magnificat, the song of Mary, taken from the Gospel according to St Luke. As Daniels joined in chanting it one evening in Cambridge, the words at the very heart of Mary's song suddenly hit the young seminarian like a freight train:

> He hath put down the mighty from their seat
> and hath exalted the humble and meek.
> He hath filled the hungry with good things,
> And the rich he hath sent empty away.

'I knew then that I must go to Selma,' Daniels later wrote, 'and the Virgin's song was to grow more and more dear in the weeks ahead.' So, rather than spending his Spring Break at Cape Cod or on Nantucket Island like the rest of the North's gilded youth, Daniels answered Dr King's call and made his way down to Selma with a group of his fellow seminarians, to observe the situation there and to offer what solidarity they could over the course of a long weekend.

It would not have been a life-changing trip were it not for the third (and easily the most prosaic) of the incidents that were to shape Daniels' ministry: he missed his bus home. The short weekend trip to observe the situation suddenly became an extended stay trapped in a violent, discriminatory part of the country where his very presence was resented. He realised that this was not just an abstract political problem but the reality of life for black Alabamans every single day. When he eventually returned to Cambridge, he immediately put in a request to spend the following semester not in the libraries and study room of the seminary but back in Selma. He described himself as 'blinded' by what he had seen there and was adamant that, for him, 'the road to Damascus' led back to Alabama.

In Alabama, Daniels wrote, 'Sometimes we take to the streets, sometimes we yawn through interminable meetings … Sometimes we confront the posse, sometimes we hold a child.' Daniels was left quite literally holding the baby a number of times, either helping to take care of the children of fellow activists or coordinating students and young people, who, though they were too young to vote, could and did protest against segregated public spaces. Daniels was to become enormously important for the eleven children in the West household of Selma. It was with the Wests that Daniels stayed for most of his time in Alabama, ensuring that the children had books, pens and paper and instilling in them his own two loves: for learning and for God.

His primary ministry in the Deep South was to be visible. He was not a senior figure like Fred Shuttlesworth or Dr King, but the sight of the neat, starch-collared young white man with his cut-glass New England accent standing and marching alongside the oppressed people of Alabama sent a profound message. It was not always a popular one, however. Daniels recalled that in a store not far from Selma, a man noticed his seminarian's garb, put two and two together and spat at him. 'So you're a white nigger, ain't you.' Daniels wore the insult with pride, as he did all his confrontations – be they with police or pastors of his own church whose congregations Daniels would often forcibly integrate.

The issue of integrated spaces was central to the civil rights struggle in Alabama. Who could sit in certain places, order certain food or use certain amenities at certain times was tightly controlled in order to emphasise the supposed inferiority of black people. As with the intricate racial cataloguing of Nazi Germany, the devil (quite literally, as far as Daniels was concerned) was in the detail. Increasingly, his presence was required to assist desegregation protests elsewhere in the troubled state. Daniels found himself making regular trips to Lowndes County, a largely rural, desperately poor county to the south-east of Selma. Lowndes was 'the rust buckle on the black belt', a strip of land across south/central Alabama famed for its rich black soil and its largely black population. As such, the maintenance of segregation in counties like Lowndes required a climate of violence and fear. The Klan was strong, lynching was common and the county at the heart of the belt acquired a new nickname: Bloody Lowndes.

It was to Fort Deposit, the largest town in Lowndes County, that Daniels, a young Roman Catholic priest called Father Richard Morrisroe and twenty-seven other protestors went on 14th August 1965. They were there to assist in the effort to desegregate a number of whites-only businesses in a protest coordinated by the Student Nonviolent Coordinating Committee, a group of young black men and women determined to make their voices heard. One of its key members in Fort Deposit was the seventeen-year-old Ruby Sales. She and Daniels had got to know one another through his regular trips to Lowndes County to lend what aid he could.

The pair had struck up a rapport that might have seemed unlikely given their differing backgrounds – Ruby was the child of a soldier and a nurse and, compared to the erudite Daniels, she felt, in her own words, like 'a peasant'. Yet a friendship was formed, largely based on mutual teasing. The bright and brilliant Daniels, always keen to instil a love of learning, would joshingly cajole Sales into discussion, correcting her when she got things wrong. Sales, confronted with the (in her words again) 'starchy' Yankee ordinand, doubtless had more than enough material with which to get back at him.

The protest in Fort Deposit turned ugly and the twenty-nine protestors were arrested. Despite Fort Deposit's size, the administrative centre of Lowndes County was, in fact, the tiny backwater town of Hayneville. Consequently, the group were loaded onto a garbage truck and, amid piles of foetid rubbish, transported to the county jail there. The next day, some protestors were released without charge, while a number, mostly white and including Daniels, were offered bail and the opportunity to leave. Daniels and his fellow protestors refused; either all were offered bail, including the black prisoners, or none were.

Eventually, after six days in prison, on 20th August, the group was tossed out onto Hayneville's dusty main thoroughfare without any prospect of a lift to Fort Deposit. While they tried to work out how to get back to a centre of comparative urbanisation, Daniels, Sales, Father Morrisroe and another black teenager, Joyce Bailey, wandered over to Varner's Cash Store for some cold drinks to keep spirits up. As they crossed the concrete step up to the small brick building, a figure appeared brandishing a shotgun. It was one Thomas Coleman, a construction worker, part-time deputy sheriff of Lowndes County and associate of the Klan.

'Get off this property,' an enraged Coleman shouted, 'or I'll blow your goddamn heads off, you sons of bitches.'

There was little time to react. Coleman swung his gun towards Sales. As he pulled the trigger, Daniels dived into the path of the bullet and, in so doing, laid down his life for Ruby Sales. Morrisroe and Bailey, a few steps behind, turned and fled. Coleman fired after them, hitting the Roman Catholic priest in the back. He then aimed his gun towards Bailey and warned that, if she helped him, she'd be shot too.

Ruby Sales only realised that she wasn't dead when she heard Joyce Bailey's cries and Father Morrisroe asking for water. Dazed by the force of the gunshot, she came to her senses and realised that Daniels had taken the full blast of Coleman's gun, so much so that his body, lying motionless like a broken doll in the Alabama dust, was almost severed in half.

Coleman wandered into the sheriff's office and turned himself in. 'I just shot two preachers,' he told his colleagues. A clean-up operation was put into action and the next day, as federal investigators put it, 'it looked as if there'd been no murder at all'. The powers that be in Lowndes County made it very clear which side they were on, even going so far as to initially refuse the release of the seminarian's body to his grieving mother. Coleman was tried by an all-white jury and acquitted of murder, with the 'twelve honest men and true' shaking hands with him as he left the court a free man. When asked some years later if he had any regrets, he replied that, given the opportunity, he'd shoot both men again.

As well as tributes from Martin Luther King and President Lyndon B. Johnson, Daniels was memorialised by the Presiding Bishop of the Episcopal Church, John Hines. Hines was young (for a bishop), newly elected and a bullish Southerner himself. His statement pulled no punches. He issued a wake-up call to the Church and the nation, saying that the murder of Daniels showed 'the fearful price extracted from society for the administration of the system by people whose prejudices lead them to sacrifice justice upon the altar of their irrational fears'. He also observed that, if the most brilliant scion of the white elite could be denied justice in Alabama, what hope did 'minorities have of securing even-handed justice'? Daniels had laid down his life, but his friends, allies and colleagues now had the task of ensuring it was not in vain. That is, undoubtedly, a process that is still ongoing in the United States of America.

While ensconced in jail, Daniels had written a note to his mother, in anticipation of her sixtieth birthday on 20th August, the very day he would be killed. It shows another side to the man – different from the earnest activist, dedicated student, or pious would-be priest who appears elsewhere. 'The food is vile', he scrawled, 'and we aren't allowed to bathe. Phew ... As you can imagine, I'll have a tale or two to swap over our next martini'. Urbane, amusing and with just a soupçon of camp, this was the young man his friends and family back in New Hampshire lost when the Church and the civil rights movement gained their saint and martyr. No more witty asides, no gentle teasing, no more Martinis – Jonathan Daniels had laid down his life, but his friends and family remained bereft. Daniels' story of bravery has its tragic note, perhaps best expressed by Ruby Sales, speaking many years later as a college professor (something that would have amused and delighted Daniels). She said of her protector's death, 'Isn't it an absolute travesty that society would kill its best and brightest when they stand up for freedom?'

In the same speech, Sales said, in reference to his privileged background and glittering prospects, that when Daniels sacrificed himself, he 'walked away from the king's table'. Yet Jonathan Daniels believed he was doing the exact opposite. His entire time in Alabama and his entire commitment to fighting racism was predicated on the fact that, for him, such unselfish love of one's fellow man was the way to the table of the king who said, 'Greater love hath no man than this, that he lay down his life for his friends.'

EPILOGUE

Strength Made Perfect in Weakness

When, in 1975, the journalist Vladimir Herzog (who had been smuggled to Brazil from Croatia as a child by his family in order to escape Nazi persecution on account of his Jewish heritage) was reported to have committed suicide, his Rabbi smelled a rat. Herzog had been living a double life as both the editor-in-chief of the São Paulo state television station and also as a leader of the civil resistance movement against the regime. The secret police had discovered Herzog's clandestine links to the opposition in October 1975 and, on the 24th of that month, summoned him for interrogation. On 25th October, the military announced that he had hanged himself with a belt in his cell.

In fact, the journalist had died while being brutally tortured by the secret police. A false autopsy report was produced and, hoping that this would silence any further questions, they allowed Herzog to be buried in São Paulo's Jewish cemetery. However, they had reckoned without two factors; firstly, Herzog's reputation as a journalist meant that questions were already being asked in the United States and Europe about the dubious circumstances surrounding his death and, secondly, the burial was to be conducted by a markedly unconventional Rabbi.

With flowing coiffed hair and a penchant for embroidered yarmulkes, Rabbi Henry Sobel had differences of both religious belief and personality with Cardinal Arns, the leader of the Brazilian Roman Catholic Church, but they both shared a fierce opposition to the regime and an eye for the impact of the dramatic act (although Sobel would later take this a little too far when he was arrested for shoplifting hundreds of dollars' worth of cravats from a store in Palm Beach, Florida). Against the express orders of the military, Sobel arranged for Herzog's body to be inspected and, having found marks of torture on the corpse, refused to inter Herzog in the corner of the Jewish burial ground reserved for suicides, instead laying him to rest slap bang in the middle of the plot so that all would know his death had been no accident.

In light of what he had discovered, Sobel contacted Cardinal Arns, suggesting that a show of unity by the nation's religious leaders might just generate the publicity needed to expose Herzog's murder for what it was. Arns agreed and offered São Paulo's Roman Catholic cathedral for a joint service to mark what had occurred. The government got wind of what was happening and sent battalions of soldiers and a detachment of tanks to surround the cathedral in order to discourage attendance. It didn't work. With nearly eight thousand people crammed into and spilling out of the church, Cardinal Arns seized his moment. Normally known for his humility (preferring a shabby cardigan and stained slippers to the flowing robes one might expect from a prince of the Church), Arns was perfectly capable of utilising the mystique of his office when required; with all eyes on his wiry frame, he made his way slowly into the pulpit, drew himself up to his full height and announced, quietly and clearly to the world, that Vladimir Herzog had not killed himself but had been tortured to death by the secret police. His address contained a direct shot at the regime, one which was to be reported all over the world: 'Those who stain their hands with blood are damned!' he cried. 'Thou shalt not kill!'

The government was incandescent and made sure that a series of death threats arrived at the little monastic cell occupied by Arns over the next few weeks. Their message was clear: if we can murder a prominent journalist, an Archbishop could be next. Arns ignored the threats and, summoning his fellow bishops, put together a statement, to be read out in churches across the country, in response to the murder of Herzog and the continued use of torture and oppression by the dictatorship. It outlined, with the crisp, pointed prose for which Arns was to become known, that despite torture being utterly contrary to the laws of God and of Man, it was happening every day in Brazil. The moment was considered a turning point; neither the international community nor the majority of Brazilians could ignore the reality of military dictatorship in Brazil any longer.

Fascist Europe was the world of eighty years ago, segregated America that of sixty years ago, dictatorship-dominated Brazil forty years ago. In the late twentieth century, we told ourselves the comforting lie that they would remain there, in the past, and yet as we career towards the end of the first quarter of the twenty-first century all those tropes look set to reappear. Fundamentally, this ought to be of no surprise. They are, after all, manifestations of human nature. At the root of the faith that the figures in this volume shared is a belief that such a nature is flawed and fallen – and yet capable of redemption. What tied Fascists together was a belief that human nature (at least, that of people who looked or spoke like them) was not flawed. They believed that people could attain purity here on earth, that they could become supermen, a master race.

What, conversely, these men and women of resistance show is the frailty of humanity. For some that was by their own manifest ridiculousness – the Pooh-like gourmand-ising of Canon Kir or the stubborn-as-a-mule character of Fred Shuttlesworth. For others it was embracing their own mortality, giving up their lives like Jane Haining or Maximilian Kolbe. Yet we would be mistaken to view these as figures of the past: across the world, from Brasilia to Budapest, men (whether they call themselves presidents or princes, generalissimos or General Secretaries) are echoing the age-old tropes once more; and others might do well to look to the lives described here for guidance on how to respond. If these examples reveal anything universal, perhaps it is a counter-intuitive truth that might is not right, that true strength is achieved in embracing our weaknesses.

Such is the vision of the Kingdom of God set out in the Sermon on the Mount. The earth, Christ teaches, will be inherited not by the strong but by 'the meek', the Kingdom of Heaven belongs not to the manifestly successful but to 'those who are persecuted for righteousness' sake'. With this vision of humanity at the centre of the worldview of the people described in this volume, it is little surprise that they opposed those who were trying to build a world of strength, cruelty and arrogance.

Theology, however, is never that simple. For every tale of bravery related above, there were tales of abject cowardice and collaboration. For every figure who discerned the true direction of oppressive regimes, there were those who continued to tell themselves that such excesses were overstated. For every man and woman of faith who identified political totalitarianism as against the will of God, there were plenty who saw it ushering in God's own Kingdom, on the left and the right. As the old Russian joke goes, 'What is the difference between Fascism and Communism? Fascism is the oppression of man by man; in Communism it is the other way round.'

Either the Kingdom is a vision that belongs to neither left nor right, either it is a vision around which everyone, from a Serene Princess of Battenberg to an unwashed French former scout leader with a persistent chesty cough, can coalesce, or it is nothing. Of course, at no point has anyone suggested such a path would be easy – indeed, a great deal of the Bible, the history of the Church and the lot of people across the world today suggests quite the opposite. The lives – and deaths – of men like Pietro Pappagallo and women like Sara Salkaházi were not ones of ease, but they were ones of integrity, of commitment to something that they believed to be higher than even those earthly powers that seemed unstoppable.

In his second letter to the Corinthians, St Paul writes of a vision he had in the midst of personal doubt in which God tells him that 'my strength is made perfect in weakness'. None of these stories is without its moments of doubt, failure and weakness. Even Canon Kir must have had a flash of doubt as he looked up from where he lay wounded at the unfinished snack on the kitchen table. Yet the moments of utmost weakness, even the ultimate act of vulnerability – giving oneself up to death – were often the moments when these individuals' principles and faith proved most strong. Strength made perfect in weakness indeed.

When I was being selected for the priesthood, one of the questions I was asked was, 'What would you go to the stake for?' In a draughty house in the middle of Staffordshire, with the unmistakable smell of bulk-bought air freshener in my nostrils and perched on a chair that was doubtless the height of mass-produced conference centre-style circa 1988 (for it is in such glamorous surroundings that our state Church chooses its future priests and prophets), the question seemed almost a ridiculous one. Yet at its root was a profound truth, namely that by working out what we are prepared to die for, we might discern what it is we want to live for. None of us wants to make the choices that these men and women were forced to make, but, as the tropes get recycled and the anger swells, it may well be that this and future generations will be asked to stand in similar shoes to the figures in this book. It can only be hoped that they have the faith to act in the same way.

I will shew thee my faith by my works.

JAMES 2:18

FURTHER READING

CANON FÉLIX KIR

There exists, most regrettably, no full-length biography of the astonishing life of Canon Kir in English. The casual reader would be best advised to garner information from cocktail recipe books – such as *Knack Bartending Basics: More than 400 Classic and Contemporary Cocktails for Any Occasion*, by the gloriously named Cheryl Charming (Rowman and Littlefield, 2009). Alternatively, for the Francophones among this book's readership, two masterful but rather different takes on Canon Kir exist in his native tongue – *Le Chanoine Kir: L'invention d'une légende* by Louis Devance (Dijon University Press, 2007) and *Le chanoine Kir: La vie fantasque d'un homme politique en soutane* by Jean-François Bazin (Armand Colin, 2018), with the latter containing some particularly marvellous pictures of Kir in action. Perhaps the best advice the author can give to the newly converted Kir enthusiast is to go, as he did, to Dijon and commune with the late canon's spirit through copious consumption of blancs de cassis.

ABBÉ PIERRE

Abbé Pierre's own collection of writings was voluminous; the cheerily titled *Why, O why, My God,* produced by the World Council of Churches just after his death in 2007, gives a flavour of his style and substance. The book that introduced Abbé Pierre's Emmaus project to the Anglosphere was undoubtedly Boris Simon's translation of Lucie Noel's French original, *Abbé Pierre and the Ragpickers of Emmaus.* It is long out of print but not impossible to get hold of and gives a good sense of the heady days of the early movement. Emmaus acts as something of a guardian of his legacy still and have plenty of information. In French, there is Pierre Lunel's marathon *Abbé Pierre: L'insurgé de Dieu* (Aripoche, 2012), which contains all the Abbé Pierre-related information – including long quotes and facsimiles of letters to the author – one could wish for. For fans of French cinema, the 1989 biopic of Pierre – *Hiver '52* is, er, quite something. After cutting his teeth playing a black-coated outcast, the film's star went on to land roles in *The Matrix Reloaded* and *The Matrix Revolutions* (both 2003). With regard to more general histories of the French Resistance, in which clergy play occasional roles – both the tales of Protestant Pastor Trocmé in Robert Gildea's masterly *Fighters in the Shadows* (Harvard University Press, 2015) and of the urbane French Jesuit Pierre Chaillet and the remarkable Ukrainian Jewish convert Abbé Glasberg in Caroline Moorehead's *Village of Secrets: Defying the Nazis in Vichy France* (Random House, 2014) are very powerful and worth discovering.

CLEMENS AUGUST, BISHOP OF MÜNSTER
AND GRAF VON GALEN

Von Galen, perhaps surprisingly for a figure who was himself so doggedly uninterested in formalised learning, has been the focus of a quite vigorous academic debate in the early years of the twenty-first century. Beth A. Griech-Polelle's strongly critical attempt to demolish the 'myth' of von Galen as a 'good German' (*Bishop von Galen: German Catholicism and National Socialism*, Yale University Press, 2002) prompted a flurry of counter-arguments. Perhaps the most brutal demolition of her case is Kevin Spicer's review in *Holocaust and Genocide Studies*, Oxford, vol. 18, no. 3, Winter 2004, which clinically points out numerous factual and chronological errors that suggest von Galen was, in fact, more impressive than his first English-language biographer since his chaplain Heinrich Portmann's panegyric *Cardinal von Galen* (trans. R. L. Sedgwick, 1957) would allow. Aside from being a scholarly take on von Galen, the review is worth reading as an example of academic shade thrown well. On the other end of the spectrum *The Lion of Münster: The Bishop who Roared Against the Nazis* (Daniel Utrecht, TAN Books, 2016) is a thoroughly modern take on the medieval hagiography. As with many figures here, von Galen is best assessed through his own words. His sermon of 3rd August as well as a contemporary account of his impact can be found in *Behind Valkyrie: German Resistance to Hitler (Documents)* (ed. P. Hoffmann, McGill University Press, 2011).

DIETRICH BONHOEFFER

Behind Valkyrie (see above) also contains much of Bonhoeffer's own writing, including his denunciation of Hitler as Führer and his decision against emigrating. Bonhoeffer's works are famous and numerous – his *Life Together* (first published 1939 and drawing on his time running the underground seminary and in print ever since) is probably the most important book on what being a Christian community means since the Rule of St Benedict was written in the mid-sixth century AD – it was compulsory reading at my theological college. Bonhoeffer's *The Cost of Discipleship* (1937, ditto still in print) is considered another classic. Neither is especially long; both are immensely powerful. Numerous English-language biographies abound – Eric Metaxas's *Bonhoeffer: Pastor, Martyr, Prophet, Spy* (HarperCollins, 2nd edition, 2012) is readable, moving and erudite.

DON PIETRO PAPPAGALLO

As with Kir, for one so well known in his homeland, there is almost nothing on Don Pietro available in English. Indeed, the author himself only discovered Pappagallo's existence when he happened upon a plaque while strolling idly down the Via Urbana when on a placement in Rome. In Italian, there is Professor Antonio Lisi's *Don Pietro Pappagallo* – published, confusingly, with interchangeable subtitles of either *un eroe, un santo* or *martire delle fosse ardeantine* (Libera Moderna, various dates) – which remains the best source (aside from various shorter biographies produced by magazines and the Church itself) for biography. It was Lisi's book that inspired the production of *La Buona Battaglia*, an enormously successful multi-part series produced by state broadcaster RAI in 2006. However, by far the best-known rendering of Don Pietro's story (albeit in a highly stylised form) is another film *Roma: Città Aperta* (Rome: Open City) a neo-realist masterpiece from 1945 by the director Roberto Rossellini, the lover of Ingrid Bergman. The film is said to be the favourite of Pope Francis.

BISHOP GORAZD OF PRAGUE

Gorazd is forever destined to occupy the role of bit-part actor in much of the writing about the wider drama of Operation Anthropoid. For readers interested in arguably the most daring plot of the Second World War, Callum MacDonald's *The Assassination of Reinhard Heydrich* (Birlinn Ltd, 2007) gives a comprehensive overview, while Jan Wiener's *The Assassination of Heydrich: Hitler's Hangman and the Czech Resistance* (Irie, 2012) offers a Czech take on the story. With regard to Gorazd himself, Orthodox hagiographies innumerable are but a click away. He also gets a mention in *Prague Panoramas: National Memory and Sacred Space in the Twentieth Century* (University of Pittsburgh Press, 2009), Cynthia Paces's beautifully written take on monuments in the Czech capital. Again, the best advice for any diehard Gorazd fans out there is to visit his cathedral – the author lived just around the corner from it while on a university year abroad. There is a well-curated exhibition, carefully preserved bullet holes and a themed restaurant with excellent beer directly opposite.

ST MAXIMILIAN KOLBE

As a result of his heroism and subsequent canonisation (and in a presumed tribute to the stylistic tendencies of much of Kolbe's own oeuvre) much that is written on Kolbe is essentially devotional biography. Of these, Cendrine Fontan's translation of André Frossard's *Forget Not Love: The Passion of Maximilian Kolbe* (Ignatius Press, 1991) tells his extraordinary tale with readable aplomb and Patricia Treece's *A Man for Others* (Marytown, 1993) does the best job of making use of original sources and contains an awful lot of detail in the words of those who knew him. With regard to his own writings, both *The Kolbe Reader* (ed. Anselm Romb OFM, Prow Books, 1987) and *Stronger than Hatred* (New City, 1988) are helpful distillations of his vast output. The most affecting link one can make with Kolbe is to take the journey to Auschwitz–Birkenau, where, unlike much of the camp, his condemned cell has survived. In it burns a single candle, a sign of hope in what is possibly the single darkest place on earth.

SISTER SÁRA SALKAHÁZI

As with some of the other figures here, Sára Salkaházi is unfortunately not widely known outside her native land and so English-language texts for further reading are few and far between. Zoltan Vagi et al.'s *The Holocaust in Hungary: Evolution of a Genocide* (AltaMira, 2013) is weightily academic but includes some powerful primary resources relating to her life and, in particular, the moments immediately before her death. Otherwise, outside Hungary itself, Salkaházi is only mentioned in even more esoteric publications – *When the War Was Over: Women, War and Peace in Europe 1940–1956* (Claire Duchen et al., Leicester University Press, 2000) and on numerous Catholic devotional sites and pamphlets, which, understandably, wish to keep her memory alive.

CARDINAL DE JONG, KOENO GRAVEMEIJER & ST EDITH STEIN

Michael Phayer's *The Catholic Church and the Holocaust 1930–1965* (Indiana University Press, 2000) – worth a read more generally for those interested in this subject – gives a good and honest account of de Jong's dilemma and clashes with Seyss-Inquart. As far as the author is aware, nothing exists in any languages other than Dutch and Afrikaans on Gravemeijer. By contrast, there exists a vast amount of work about and by Edith Stein. Her unfinished autobiography, *Life in a Jewish Family* (trans. Josephine Koeppel OCB, ICS, 1999), is certainly worth reading, as are, for the academically minded reader, her other collected works, with *The Hidden Life* being a particularly moving piece of religious writing and *Essays on Woman* marking her out as a writer of impressive prose beyond that of a purely devotional nature.

MOTHER SUPERIOR ALICE-ELIZABETH, PRINCESS ANDREW OF GREECE AND DENMARK

Undoubtedly the finest work on Alice is Hugo Vickers's erudite, witty and compassionate treatment of the nun-Princess *Alice: Princess Andrew of Greece* (St Martin's Press, reissue, 2013). Inevitably, much of Alice's story has been told in relation to the life of her son – Philip Eade's *Young Prince Philip* (HarperCollins, 2011) is readable throughout and the figure of Alice, inevitably, plays a key role. For the cinematically inclined, Channel 4's 2012 documentary *The Queen's Mother-in-Law*, although verging at points on a dramatisation, gives a clear sense of the enormous character of Princess Andrew and is as good a start as any for any budding Alice enthusiast.

ARCHBISHOP DAMASKINOS OF ATHENS AND ALL GREECE

For a figure so crucial in his own nation's past, Damaskinos gets little or no attention from writers in English. Aside from the odd paragraph in histories of Greece at the time (Rigas Rigopoulos's *Secret War: Greece – Middle East 1940–45*, 2003) or histories of the Holocaust (such as Betty N. Hoffmann's *Liberation: Stories of Survival from the Holocaust*, 1998 – the United States Holocaust Memorial Museum and, of course, Yad Vashem, have excellent resources online about him) he barely features. One obvious exception to this is in Churchill's writings, where he details 'Christmas at Athens' in chapter 19 of volume six of his history of the Second World War (entitled *Triumph and Tragedy*).

MONSIGNOR HUGH O'FLAHERTY

A large corpus of work exists on O'Flaherty, the result of him being (despite his own views on the Anglosphere) an English speaker and, of course, due to his riveting story. J. P. Gallagher's *Scarlet Pimpernel of the Vatican* (HarperCollins, reprints since 1967) was the book that brought O'Flaherty's story to the world and, of course, was the direct inspiration for *The Scarlet and the Black* (1983). More recently, Brian Fleming's *The Vatican Pimpernel* (Skyhorse, 2012) is a good contemporary account of O'Flaherty's heroism and is well worth a read. If the reader is interested in the general atmosphere around the Vatican during the Second World War, I would recommened Owen Chadwick's masterful *Britain and the Vatican during the Second World War* (CUP, 1988). Although it sounds like it should be a dry diplomatic history, it is in fact a riotously readable recounting of the exploits of O'Flaherty, Sir D'Arcy Osborne et al.

JANE HAINING

It was former Prime Minister Gordon Brown's *Wartime Courage: Stories of Extraordinary Courage by Ordinary People in World War Two* (Bloomsbury, 2008) that really brought Haining to the attention of many in Britain. Despite the clunky, Broonian title, his section on Haining is worth a read. Naturally, it sparked a number of other Haining-related books, including Lynley Smith's *From Matron to Martyr* (Zaccmedia, 2017). For a more academic source, *The Holocaust in Hungary* (see Sister Sára Salkaházi above) also contains primary documentary sources about Jane's time in

Budapest. The website of the little church in Dunscore has a rather sweet subsection dedicated entirely to Jane and her efforts. The memorial to her there is also very affecting and very much worth a visit.

PASTOR FRED SHUTTLESWORTH

Though not as much has been written on Shuttlesworth as on men like Dr King and Jesse Jackson, there is a healthy corpus of publications dedicated to study of his life and work. Much of it is the work of Andrew M. Manis, a scholar at Macon State College who has written a great deal on the role of religion in the civil rights movement. His 2001 work, *A Fire You Can't Put Out* (University of Alabama Press) and his joint editing of a collection of essays entitled *Birmingham Revolutionaries* with Marjorie White (Mercer, 2000) both stand out. More recently, L. D. Brimner's *Black & White: The Confrontation between Reverend Fred Shuttlesworth and Eugene "Bull" Connor* (Calkins Creek, 2011) throws a specific focus on the animosity at the heart of Birmingham in the 1960s.

SEMINARIAN JONATHAN DANIELS

Jonathan Daniels is now in the calendar (the closest Anglicans get to canonisation these days) of the Episcopal Church and there are numerous very good devotional and online resources relating his story. Surprisingly, given the prominence he is given in a number of Anglican circles

(Presiding Bishop Michael Curry of 2018 royal wedding fame has preached on his story a number of times), there are very few books about his life. Perhaps the most interesting of the small selection is a book aimed at young adults entitled *Blood Brother* (Highlights Press, 2016) by Rich and Sandra Neil Wallace, which, although with some dramatic licence, tells the tale sensitively and powerfully.

The Reverend Fergus Butler-Gallie is a clergyman who has served in London and Liverpool and the author of *A Field Guide to the English Clergy*, a Best Book of the Year for *The Times*, *Mail on Sunday* and *BBC History*. This is his second book.